Mastering Business English

Unlocking Powerful Idioms, Sayings, and Expressions to Build Your Vocabulary for Success!

Simon Tracey

Copyright © 2025 by Simon Tracey

All rights reserved.

No portion of this book may be reproduced in any form without written permission from the publisher or author, except as permitted by U.S. copyright law.

Contents

Introduction	1
1. Communicating with Clarity and Confidence	8
2. Emails That Get Results	15
3. Participating in Meetings with Confidence	22
4. Managing Projects and Discussing Progress	31
5. Navigating Difficult Conversations and Constructive Feedback	41
6. Winning Job Interviews	50
7. Networking Like a Pro	60
8. Public Speaking and Powerful Presentations	70
9. Leading with Impactful Language	82
10. Negotiating and Persuading Successfully	93
11. Excelling in International Business	104
12. Communicating Effectively in a Virtual World	115
13. Quick-Reference Glossary	126
14. A-Z Glossary	143
15. Interactive Learning Section (Bonus)	192

16. Your Journey Toward Mastery 208

Introduction
Building Rapport and Making Connections

Welcome to the first step in transforming your professional communication. Building rapport—the art of creating a positive, mutual connection with others—is the foundation of all successful business relationships. It's what turns a cold contact into a warm lead, a tense negotiation into a collaborative discussion, and a group of colleagues into a productive team. In this chapter, you will learn the essential phrases and expressions that help you move beyond robotic greetings and build genuine, lasting professional relationships. Mastering these will enable you to start conversations with confidence, navigate small talk gracefully, and make requests in a way that gets positive results.

Essential Expressions for Building Rapport

Here are the key phrases for making introductions, engaging in small talk, and making polite requests. Each is explained with a simple definition and a realistic usage example.

1. Greetings and Introductions

These phrases are your entry point into any professional conversation. They set the tone for the entire interaction.

- **Expression:** "It's a pleasure to meet you." / "A pleasure to meet you."

  - **Explanation:** A classic and professional way to greet someone for the first time. It's warmer and more formal than "Nice to meet you."

  - **Example:** "Hello, I'm Sarah from the marketing department. It's a pleasure to meet you."

- **Expression:** "I've heard great things about your work."

  - **Explanation:** A powerful phrase used when meeting someone whose reputation you know. It's a sincere compliment that shows you've done your homework.

  - **Example:** "David, it's a pleasure to finally meet you. I've heard great things about your work on the new software launch."

- **Expression:** "Thanks for making the time to meet with me."

  - **Explanation:** A polite and respectful way to open a meeting, acknowledging that the other person's time is valuable.

  - **Example:** "Good morning, Ms. Chen. Thanks for making the time to meet with me today. I know how busy you are."

- **Alex:** "Excuse me, you're Dr. Evans, right? I'm Alex Lee. I've been following your research on supply chain management for years." **Dr. Evans:** "Oh, please, call me Susan. It's a pleasure to meet you, Alex." **Alex:** "Likewise. I've heard great things about your work from my colleagues at Innovate Corp." **Dr. Evans:**

"That's kind of you to say. It's always great to connect with people in the field."**Scenario: Attending a Conference**

2. Engaging in Small Talk

Small talk is the bridge from introduction to business. It's how you find common ground and show you're interested in the other person, not just the transaction.

- **Expression:** "How has your week been so far?"
    - **Explanation:** A simple, open-ended question that invites more than a "yes" or "no" answer. It's a safe and professional way to start a conversation.
    - **Example:** (Waiting for a meeting to start) "Hi, Tom. How has your week been so far? Anything exciting?"
- **Expression:** "So, what do you do at [Company Name]?"
    - **Explanation:** A direct but polite way to understand someone's role. The "So" at the beginning makes it sound more conversational.
    - **Example:** "It's great to connect, Maria. So, what do you do at Apex Solutions? I'm in the sales division."
- **Expression:** "I hear you're a fan of [Hobby/Interest]."
    - **Explanation:** Use this when you know a small piece of personal information. It shows you listen and remember, which is excellent for building rapport.

- **Example:** "Before we start, John, I hear you're a fan of hiking. I saw some pictures from your trip to the mountains on LinkedIn—it looked amazing."

- **Priya:** "Good morning, Ken. Thanks for making the time to chat."**Ken:** "Of course, Priya. How has your week been so far?"**Priya:** "It's been productive, thanks. We're getting ready for the product showcase next month. And you?"**Ken:** "Same here, lots to do. By the way, I saw on your profile that you used to work at TechFirm. I know a few people there."**Priya:** "Oh, really? It's a small world! It was a great place to start my career."**Scenario: Making Conversation Before a Meeting**

3. Making Polite Requests

How you ask for something is just as important as what you ask for. These phrases soften your requests and increase your chances of a "yes."

- **Expression:** "I was wondering if you could…"

  - **Explanation:** A very common and polite way to frame a request. It's indirect and less demanding than "Can you…"

  - **Example:** "Hi, Sarah. I was wondering if you could send me the report from yesterday's meeting when you have a moment."

- **Expression:** "Would you be able to…?"

  - **Explanation:** Another gentle and professional way to ask for help or an action. It gives the other person an easy way to decline if they are unable to help.

- **Example:** "Hi, Mark. Would you be able to look over this presentation slide for me? I'd appreciate a second pair of eyes."

* **Expression:** "No worries if not."

  - **Explanation:** This is a fantastic phrase to add to the end of a request. It takes the pressure off the other person and shows you respect their time and priorities.

  - **Example:** "Hi, Jen. I was wondering if you could introduce me to your contact at Global Imports? No worries if not, but I thought I'd ask."

* **Liam:** "Hey, Chloe. Do you have a second?" **Chloe:** "Sure, Liam. What's up?" **Liam:** "I'm working on the quarterly budget forecast, and I'm having trouble with a formula in Excel. I know you're a wizard at this stuff. Would you be able to take a quick look?" **Chloe:** "I have a meeting in five, but I can stop by your desk afterward." **Liam:** "That would be amazing, thank you. But if you're swamped, no worries if not. I can try asking someone else." **Chloe:** "No, it's fine! I'm happy to help. See you in a bit." **Scenario: Asking a Colleague for Help**

Common Mistakes and How to Avoid Them

* **Mistake 1: Skipping Small Talk.** Jumping directly into business can feel abrupt and cold, especially in Western cultures.

  - **How to Avoid:** Always dedicate a minute or two to simple, friendly conversation ("How was your weekend?" "How's your day going?") before diving into the main topic.

- **Mistake 2: Being Too Personal.** Asking about sensitive topics like salary, politics, religion, or age is unprofessional and can make people uncomfortable.
  - **How to Avoid:** Stick to safe, neutral topics like work, recent projects, hobbies, travel, or weekend plans.

- **Mistake 3: Making Demands, Not Requests.** Phrasing a request as a command (e.g., "I need you to send me the file") can create resentment.
  - **How to Avoid:** Always soften your requests with phrases like "I was wondering if..." or "Would you mind...?" It shows respect for the other person's autonomy.

Try This: Your Turn to Practice

Here is a mini-scenario. Read it and think about how you would respond using the phrases from this chapter.**Scenario:** You are at a company-wide networking event. You see a senior manager from a department you'd like to work in someday. You have never spoken to her before, but you know her name is Maria. She is standing alone for a moment.**Your Task:**

1. How would you approach and introduce yourself to Maria?

2. What is one "small talk" question you could ask to start a conversation?

3. Imagine the conversation goes well. How would you politely ask if she would be open to a 15-minute chat next week to discuss her department?

(Think about your answers, or even say them out loud. Compare them to the phrases we covered. For example: "Excuse me, Maria? My name is [Your Name]... It's a pleasure to meet you. I've heard great things about the work your team is doing...")

Chapter 1: Key Takeaways

First Impressions Matter: Start conversations with warm, professional greetings like "It's a pleasure to meet you."

Small Talk Builds Bridges: Use simple, open-ended questions about work or neutral topics to build a connection before getting to business.

Politeness Pays Off: Frame your requests softly using phrases like "I was wondering if..." and "Would you be able to...?" to show respect.

Avoid Common Pitfalls: Don't skip small talk, get too personal, or make demands instead of requests.

CHAPTER ONE

Communicating with Clarity and Confidence

Once you've built initial rapport, the next step is to communicate your ideas with clarity and confidence. In business, ambiguity leads to mistakes, missed deadlines, and misunderstandings. Clear communication, on the other hand, ensures everyone is aligned, projects run smoothly, and you are seen as a reliable and competent professional. This chapter provides the essential expressions you need to state your message clearly, confirm you've understood others, and interact with confidence. Using these phrases will help you eliminate confusion and project an image of someone who is both clear-headed and in control.

Essential Expressions for Clarity and Confidence

Here are the key phrases for expressing yourself clearly, confirming information, and interacting with confidence. Each is explained with a simple definition and a realistic usage example.

1. Stating Your Message with Clarity

These phrases help you structure your thoughts and present them in a way that is easy for others to understand.

Expression: "In short..." / "To put it simply..."

- **Explanation:** Use this to summarize a complex idea or get to the most important point quickly. It signals to the listener that you are providing the main takeaway.

- **Example:** "The market analysis is quite detailed, but **in short**, we're seeing a major opportunity in the Asian market."

Expression: "The bottom line is..."

- **Explanation:** This is a direct and confident phrase used to state the single most important fact or conclusion. It's often used when you want to cut through discussion and focus on a final result.

- **Example:** "We can discuss different marketing strategies all day, but **the bottom line is** we need to increase sales by 10% this quarter."

Expression: "To be clear..."

- **Explanation:** Use this phrase just before stating something you want to ensure there is absolutely no misunderstanding about. It adds emphasis and signals importance.

- **Example:** "I think we can meet the new deadline. But, **to be clear**, this means we'll need everyone working on Saturday."

- **Manager:** "Can you give us an update on the website redesign project, David?" **David:** "Of course. We've hit a few technical issues with the new database integration, which is causing a slight delay." **Manager:** "So what does that mean for the launch date?"**David:** "**The bottom line is** that the launch will be pushed back by one week. **To be clear**, the original launch was set for May 1st; the new launch date is May 8th. **To put it simply**, we need one extra week to ensure everything works perfectly."**Scenario: Team Meeting Update**

2. Confirming Understanding

These expressions are crucial for ensuring you and your conversation partner are on the same page. They prevent mistakes before they happen.

Expression: "So, if I understand correctly..."

- **Explanation:** The best way to confirm you have understood someone. You follow this phrase by restating their point in your own words.

- **Example:** "**So, if I understand correctly**, you need me to finish the draft by tomorrow, but the final version isn't due until Friday. Is that right?"

Expression: "Let me just repeat that back to you to make sure I have it right."

- **Explanation:** A slightly more formal and very thorough way to confirm details, especially for important instructions or numbers.

- **Example:** "The client's order number is 8-6-7-5-3-0-9. **Let me just repeat that back to you to make sure I have it right:** eight, six, seven, five, three, zero, nine."

Expression: "Are we on the same page?"

- **Explanation:** A conversational way to ask if everyone agrees or understands the situation in the same way. It fosters a sense of alignment.

- **Example:** "So, the plan is to focus on marketing for the first month and then shift to sales in the second month. **Are we on the same page?**"

- **Sarah:** "Okay, that was a productive call with the client."**Tom:** "Definitely. So, just to be sure we're aligned, what are the next steps?"**Sarah: "So, if I understand correctly**, we need to send them the revised proposal by end-of-day today, and they will get back to us with their feedback by the end of the week."**Tom:** "That's exactly right. I'll work on the revisions now."**Sarah:** "Perfect. So we're on the same page. Let's get it done."**Scenario: Mini-Dialogue After a Client Call**

3. Interacting with Confidence

These phrases help you manage conversations, handle questions, and project self-assurance.

Expression: "That's a great question."

- **Explanation:** A classic and effective way to respond to a difficult question. It gives you a moment to think and shows you value the person who asked.

- **Example:** (During a presentation) **Audience Member:** "How will this new strategy affect our existing clients?" **Presenter: "That's a great question.** We have a transition plan in place to ensure a smooth experience for all current clients."

Expression: "My thinking on this is..."

- **Explanation:** A confident way to introduce your opinion or perspective without sounding aggressive. It's collaborative while still being assertive.

- **Example:** "There are a few ways we could approach this. **My thinking on this is** that we should prioritize the user experience first and foremost."

Expression: "I'm confident that..."

- **Explanation:** A strong, direct phrase to show you believe in a certain outcome or in your team's ability to deliver.

- **Example:** "I know the timeline is tight, but **I'm confident that** our team can deliver the project on time."

Team Lead: "The client isn't happy with the latest design. They feel it's too generic. Any ideas?" **Maria:** "**My thinking on this is** that we've been playing it too safe. We should present them with the more innovative 'Concept B' we discussed." **Team Lead:** "That's a risk. What if they hate it?" **Maria:** "It's a possibility, but based on my previous conversations with them about wanting to be a market leader, **I'm confident that** they will appreciate a bolder approach." **Scenario: A Confident Team Contribution**

Common Mistakes and How to Avoid Them

Mistake 1: Using Filler Words. Using words like "um," "uh," "like," and "you know" can make you sound uncertain and unprofessional.

- **How to Avoid:** It's better to pause silently for a moment to collect your thoughts than to use a filler word. Practice speaking slowly and deliberately. Using phrases like "That's a great question" can also help you buy time.

Mistake 2: Upspeak. This is when you end a statement with a rising intonation, making it sound like a question. It can undermine your authority and make you sound insecure.

- **How to Avoid:** Be conscious of your tone. When making a statement, ensure your voice goes down at the end. Record yourself speaking to see if you have this habit.

Mistake 3: Assuming People Understand. Rushing through complex information without checking for understanding can lead to major problems later.

- **How to Avoid:** After explaining something important, pause and use a confirmation phrase like, "Does that make sense?" or "Are we on the same page?" to ensure alignment.

Try This: Your Turn to Practice

Scenario: Your manager has just given you verbal instructions for a new, important task. She spoke very quickly. She wants you to (1) analyze the sales data from the last quarter, (2) create a presentation with the top three key findings, and (3) email it to the entire leadership team by Thursday. **Your Task:**

1. How would you confirm the instructions back to her to ensure you understood everything correctly? Use a phrase like "So, if I understand correctly..."

2. She then asks, "Do you think you can handle this?" How would you respond with a phrase that shows confidence?

(Practice your response. For example: "Okay, so if I understand correctly, you need me to analyze the Q3 sales data, build a slide deck on the top three findings, and send it to the leadership team by Thursday. Is that right?" Followed by: "Yes, absolutely. I'm confident I can get that done.")

Chapter 2: Key Takeaways

Be Direct and Simple: Use phrases like "The bottom line is..." or "In short..." to deliver your main point clearly.

Always Confirm: Prevent misunderstandings by repeating information back using phrases like "So, if I understand correctly..."

Project Confidence: Use phrases like "I'm confident that..." and "My thinking on this is..." to sound assertive and in control.

Speak Deliberately: Avoid filler words and "upspeak" to sound more professional and authoritative.

CHAPTER TWO

Emails That Get Results

In the modern workplace, your emails are often your digital handshake, your progress report, and your professional record all in one. An email that is clear, professional, and purposeful can get you the response you need, build trust with colleagues, and solve problems efficiently. A poorly written one can cause confusion, project a lack of professionalism, or simply get ignored. This chapter focuses on the essential phrases and expressions that will transform your emails into powerful communication tools. You will learn how to write effective subject lines, structure professional messages, send polite follow-ups, and handle difficult topics with confidence and care.

Essential Expressions for Professional Emails

Here are key phrases for every part of the email process, from the subject line to the sign-off. Each is explained with a simple definition and a realistic usage example.

1. Crafting Clear and Actionable Subject Lines

The subject line is the most important part of your email. It determines if your email gets opened, prioritized, or ignored.

Format: [Topic] - [Action Required/For Your Information]

- **Explanation:** A highly effective formula for professional subject lines. It tells the reader the topic and what is expected of them.

- **Examples:**
  - "Q4 Marketing Budget - Approval Needed by Friday"
  - "Team Meeting Summary - For Your Information (FYI)"
  - "Project Phoenix Update - Action Required: Review New Timeline"

2. Professional Openings and Context

The opening of your email should be polite and get straight to the point.

Expression: "I hope this email finds you well."

- **Explanation:** A polite, slightly formal opening that is always a safe and professional choice, especially when emailing someone you don't know well.

- **Example:** "Dear Mr. Jones, I hope this email finds you well. I am writing to follow up on our conversation from last week."

Expression: "As we discussed..." / "Following up on our conversation..."

- **Explanation:** Use this to connect your email to a previous conversation. It immediately provides context for the reader.

- **Example:** "**As we discussed** in this morning's meeting, I have attached the draft proposal for your review."

Expression: "I'm writing to..." [inquire about/request/inform you that]

- **Explanation:** A clear and direct way to state the purpose of your email in the very first sentence.

- **Example:** "**I'm writing to inquire about** the status of the invoice #5821."

3. Making Requests and Attaching Documents

These phrases help you ask for things politely and refer to attachments clearly.

Expression: "Could you please...?"

- **Explanation:** A universally polite and professional way to ask the recipient to do something. It is softer than "Please..."

- **Example:** "**Could you please** let me know your availability for a brief call next week?"

Expression: "Please find attached..." / "I've attached..."

- **Explanation:** The standard way to let the reader know you have included a file with the email. "I've attached" is slightly more modern and conversational.

- **Example:** "**Please find attached** the meeting agenda. / **I've attached** the meeting agenda for your review."

4. Follow-ups and Gentle Reminders

Following up is a delicate art. These phrases help you send reminders without sounding impatient or aggressive.

Expression: "Just a gentle reminder that..."

- **Explanation:** A perfect phrase for a polite follow-up. The word "gentle" softens the reminder and shows respect for the recipient's busy schedule.

- **Example:** (In a reply to the original email) "Hi team, **just a gentle reminder that** feedback on this document is due by tomorrow."

Expression: "I was wondering if you've had a chance to..."

- **Explanation:** An indirect and very polite way to ask for an update on a previous request.

- **Example:** "Hi Ken, **I was wondering if you've had a chance to** look over the contract I sent last week."

5. Professional Closings

How you end your email leaves a final impression.

Expression: "I look forward to hearing from you."

- **Explanation:** A standard and professional closing that signals you are expecting a response.

- **Example:** "Could you please let me know your thoughts when you have a moment? **I look forward to hearing from you.**"

Expression: "Best regards," / "Kind regards,"

- **Explanation:** These are safe, professional, and friendly sign-offs that are appropriate for almost any business context. "Best regards" is neutral, while "Kind regards" is a bit warmer.

- Best regards,Sarah Chen

Short Email Example / Template

Here is a sample email that puts several of these phrases together.

Subject: Project Alpha – Action Required: Feedback on Draft

Hi Team,

I hope this email finds you well.

Following up on our meeting this morning, I've attached the draft proposal for Project Alpha.

Could you please review the document—particularly the timeline on page 3—and share any feedback by end of day Thursday?

Looking forward to your thoughts.

Best regards,

Alex

Common Mistakes and How to Avoid Them

Mistake 1: Vague Subject Lines. A subject like "Question" or "Update" is not helpful and can be easily overlooked in a crowded inbox.

- **How to Avoid:** Always be specific. Include the project name and the purpose of the email (e.g., "Project Zeta - Question about Q3 budget").

Mistake 2: Being Too Casual. Using slang, emojis, or overly casual language ("hey guys," "thx") can come across as unprofessional, especially with clients or senior management.

- **How to Avoid:** When in doubt, err on the side of formality. Use professional greetings and sign-offs like "Dear..." and "Best regards,".

Mistake 3: Writing a Wall of Text. Long, unbroken paragraphs are difficult to read on a screen and can cause your reader to miss the main point.

- **How to Avoid:** Keep your paragraphs short (2-3 sentences). Use bullet points or numbered lists to break up information and make it easy to scan.

Try This: Your Turn to Practice

Scenario: You sent an important report to your manager, John, three days ago. You needed his approval before you could send it to the client. He has not responded yet, and the client deadline is approaching.**Your Task:**Write a short, polite follow-up email to John. Your goal is to gently remind him to review the report without sounding pushy or impatient.*(Think about your response. A good email would have a clear subject line, refer to the previous email, and use a polite reminder phrase. For example: Subject: "Re: Report for Client X Approval". Body: "Hi John, I was wondering if you've had a chance to review the report for Client X I sent over on Monday? Just a gentle reminder that the client is expecting it by Friday. Please let me know if you have any questions. Best regards, [Your Name]")*

Chapter 3: Key Takeaways

Lead with the Subject: Write clear, actionable subject lines so your reader knows the topic and what you need from them immediately.

State Your Purpose Early: Begin your email by stating why you are writing (e.g., "I'm writing to request...").

Follow Up Politely: Use "gentle reminders" and indirect questions ("I was wondering if...") to check on requests without being aggressive.

Keep it Clean and Professional: Avoid overly casual language and break up long blocks of text with short paragraphs and bullet points.

Chapter Three

Participating in Meetings with Confidence

Meetings are where decisions get made, ideas are shared, and careers are built. Whether you're in a small team huddle or a large boardroom presentation, your ability to participate effectively can set you apart as a valuable team member and a future leader. However, many professionals struggle with meeting dynamics—they either stay silent and miss opportunities to contribute, or they speak up but struggle to express their ideas clearly and diplomatically. This chapter provides you with the essential phrases and expressions to participate in meetings with confidence. You will learn how to agree and disagree professionally, ask for clarification when needed, and contribute your ideas in a way that adds value to the discussion.

Essential Expressions for Meeting Participation

Here are the key phrases for every aspect of meeting participation, from agreeing with colleagues to diplomatically challenging ideas. Each is explained with a simple definition and a realistic usage example.

1. Agreeing and Supporting Ideas

These phrases help you show support for others' ideas while adding your own perspective.

Expression: "I completely agree with [Name]."

- **Explanation:** A strong, clear way to show support for someone's point. Using the person's name makes it more personal and shows you were actively listening.

- **Example:** "**I completely agree with Sarah.** The customer feedback data clearly supports this direction."

Expression: "That's exactly my thinking." / "That's exactly what I was thinking."

- **Explanation:** A conversational way to show strong agreement while indicating you had similar thoughts. It shows you're aligned and thinking strategically.

- **Example:** "**That's exactly my thinking.** We need to focus on the mobile experience first, then worry about desktop later."

Expression: "Building on what [Name] said..."

- **Explanation:** Perfect for when you agree with someone but want to add additional information or take the idea further. It shows collaboration and teamwork.

- **Example:** "**Building on what Tom said** about the budget concerns, I think we should also consider the timeline implications."

Scenario: Team Strategy Meeting

Manager: "I think we should prioritize the European market expansion this quarter." **Lisa:** "**I completely agree with you.** The market research shows strong demand there." **David:** "**Building on what Lisa said**, I've been looking at the competitive landscape in Europe, and there's definitely a gap we can fill." **Manager:** "Great. So we're all aligned on this direction."

2. Disagreeing Diplomatically

Disagreeing in meetings requires tact. These phrases help you challenge ideas respectfully without creating conflict.

Expression: "I see your point, but..."

- **Explanation:** A diplomatic way to acknowledge someone's perspective before presenting a different view. It shows respect while introducing disagreement.

- **Example:** "**I see your point, but** I'm concerned about the timeline. Three weeks might not be enough to do this properly."

Expression: "I have a slightly different perspective on this."

- **Explanation:** A gentle way to introduce disagreement without directly contradicting someone. The word "slightly" softens the disagreement.

- **Example:** "I have a slightly different perspective on this. While the cost savings are attractive, I think we need to consider the quality implications."

Expression: "Have we considered...?"

- **Explanation:** An indirect way to challenge an idea by suggesting an alternative or pointing out something that might have been overlooked.

- **Example:** "This sounds like a solid plan. **Have we considered** how this might affect our existing customers?"

Scenario: Budget Discussion

CFO: "I think we should cut the training budget by 30% to meet our targets." **HR Director:** "**I see your point** about needing to reduce costs, **but** I'm concerned that cutting training could hurt employee retention." **CFO:** "What do you mean?" **HR Director:** "**Have we considered** the cost of replacing employees who leave because they feel we're not investing in their development?"

3. Asking for Clarification

Don't be afraid to ask questions. These phrases help you get the information you need without sounding confused or unprepared.

Expression: "Could you elaborate on that?"

- **Explanation:** A professional way to ask someone to provide more detail about their point. It shows you're engaged and want to understand fully.

- **Example:** "That's an interesting approach, Mark. **Could you elaborate on** how you see this working in practice?"

Expression: "I want to make sure I understand..."

- **Explanation:** A respectful way to ask for clarification that shows you're taking the discussion seriously and want to be sure you're following correctly.

- **Example:** "**I want to make sure I understand** the timeline. Are you saying we need to have the prototype ready by the end of next week?"

Expression: "Can you walk us through...?"

- **Explanation:** Perfect for asking someone to explain a process, plan, or complex idea step by step. It's collaborative and shows you value their expertise.

- **Example:** "This sounds promising, Jennifer. **Can you walk us through** how the implementation would work?"

4. Contributing Your Ideas

These phrases help you introduce your own thoughts and suggestions confidently.

Expression: "I'd like to suggest..."

- **Explanation:** A clear, professional way to introduce your own idea or proposal. It's direct but not aggressive.

- **Example:** "**I'd like to suggest** that we run a pilot program with a small group of customers before the full launch."

Expression: "What if we...?"

- **Explanation:** A collaborative way to propose an alternative or new idea. It invites discussion rather than demanding acceptance.

- **Example:** "**What if we** approached this from the customer's perspective instead? What would they want to see?"

Expression: "From my experience..."

- **Explanation:** A confident way to share insights based on your background or expertise. It adds credibility to your contribution.

- **Example:** "**From my experience** working with similar clients, they usually prefer a phased approach rather than a big-bang implementation."

Scenario: Product Development Meeting

Product Manager: "We're trying to decide on the features for version 2.0." **Developer:** "**I'd like to suggest** that we focus on performance improvements first. The current version is getting slow with large datasets." **Designer:** "**What if we** also looked at the user interface? I've been getting feedback that it's not intuitive." **Product Manager:** "Both good points. Sarah, **from your experience** with customer support, what are you hearing?"

Common Mistakes and How to Avoid Them

Mistake 1: Staying Silent. Many people avoid speaking up in meetings because they're afraid of saying the wrong thing, but silence can be interpreted as disengagement or lack of ideas.

- **How to Avoid:** Prepare at least one question or comment before every meeting. Even asking for clarification shows you're engaged and thinking critically.

Mistake 2: Interrupting Others. Cutting people off mid-sentence is rude and can damage relationships, even if your point is valuable.

- **How to Avoid:** Wait for natural pauses, use phrases like "May I add something?" or take notes and wait for an appropriate moment to contribute.

Mistake 3: Being Too Direct with Disagreement. Saying "That's wrong" or "I disagree" without softening the language can create tension and make others defensive.

- **How to Avoid:** Always acknowledge the other person's perspective first ("I see your point...") before presenting your different view.

Try This: Your Turn to Practice

Scenario: You're in a marketing meeting. Your colleague suggests launching a new social media campaign targeting teenagers. You think this is the wrong demographic for your product, which is primarily used by working professionals aged 25-45.

Your Task:

1. How would you diplomatically disagree with your colleague's suggestion?

2. How would you introduce your alternative idea about targeting working professionals?

3. What question could you ask to get more information about their reasoning?

(Practice your responses. For example: "I see your point about social media engagement, but I have a slightly different perspective on the target demographic..." followed by "What if we focused on LinkedIn and professional networks instead?" and "Could you elaborate on why you think teenagers would be interested in our product?")

Chapter 4: Key Takeaways

Show Active Engagement: Use phrases like "I completely agree with [Name]" and "Building on what [Name] said" to demonstrate you're listening and thinking.

Disagree Diplomatically: Always acknowledge others' perspectives with "I see your point, but..." before presenting alternative views.

Ask Smart Questions: Use "Could you elaborate on that?" and "Can you walk us through...?" to get clarity and show engagement.

Contribute Confidently: Introduce your ideas with "I'd like to suggest..." and "What if we..." to add value to the discussion.

CHAPTER FOUR

Managing Projects and Discussing Progress

Project management is at the heart of modern business, and your ability to communicate effectively about projects can make the difference between success and failure. Whether you're leading a team, contributing to a project, or simply keeping stakeholders informed, the language you use to discuss timelines, delegate tasks, and report progress directly impacts how smoothly things run. Clear project communication prevents misunderstandings, keeps everyone aligned, and helps teams navigate challenges together. This chapter provides you with the essential phrases and expressions for every aspect of project communication. You will learn how to delegate tasks clearly, provide meaningful progress updates, discuss deadlines realistically, and work collaboratively to solve problems when they arise.

Essential Expressions for Project Management

Here are the key phrases for every aspect of project communication, from assigning tasks to reporting status updates. Each is explained with a simple definition and a realistic usage example.

1. Delegating Tasks and Assigning Responsibilities

These phrases help you assign work clearly and ensure everyone knows what is expected of them.

Expression: "Could you take the lead on...?"

- **Explanation:** A polite way to assign someone primary responsibility for a task or project component. It shows trust in their abilities.

- **Example:** "Sarah, **could you take the lead on** the customer research phase? You have the best relationship with our key clients."

Expression: "I'd like you to handle..."

- **Explanation:** A direct but respectful way to assign a specific task. It's clear about expectations while maintaining a collaborative tone.

- **Example:** "Mike, **I'd like you to handle** the technical documentation. You know the system better than anyone."

Expression: "This would be right up your alley."

- **Explanation:** An encouraging way to assign a task that matches someone's skills or interests. It shows you recognize their expertise.

- **Example:** "We need someone to design the user interface. Lisa, **this would be right up your alley** given your background in UX design."

Scenario: Project Kickoff Meeting

Project Manager: "Okay, let's divide up the responsibilities for the website redesign project." **Project Manager:** "Tom, **could you take the lead on** the content strategy? You did an excellent job on the last campaign." **Tom:** "Absolutely, I'd be happy to." **Project Manager:** "Great. And Jennifer, **I'd like you to handle** the technical requirements gathering. **This would be right up your alley** with your development background." **Jennifer:** "Sounds good. When do you need the initial requirements?"

2. Reporting Progress and Status Updates

These expressions help you communicate where things stand clearly and professionally.

Expression: "We're on track to..."

- **Explanation:** A positive way to report that a project is progressing as planned toward a specific goal or deadline.
- **Example:** "The development phase is going well. **We're on track to** complete the beta version by the end of next week."

Expression: "We've hit a snag with..."

33

- **Explanation:** A professional way to report a problem or obstacle without sounding overly dramatic. "Snag" suggests it's manageable.

- **Example:** "**We've hit a snag with** the database integration. The API isn't working as expected, but the vendor is working on a fix."

Expression: "We're ahead of schedule" / "We're behind schedule"

- **Explanation:** Clear, direct ways to report timing status. Being specific about schedule status helps with planning and resource allocation.

- **Example:** "Good news - the design phase is complete and **we're ahead of schedule**. We can start development earlier than planned."

Expression: "The bottleneck is..."

- **Explanation:** A business term for identifying what is slowing down progress. It helps focus problem-solving efforts on the right area.

- **Example:** "**The bottleneck is** getting approval from the legal team. Everything else is ready to go."

Scenario: Weekly Status Meeting

Manager: "How's the mobile app project coming along?" **Developer:** "Overall, **we're on track to** meet the launch date. The user interface is complete and **we're ahead of schedule** on that front." **Manager:** "That's great news. Any challenges?" **Developer:** "**We've hit a snag with** the payment integration. **The bottleneck is** waiting for the payment processor to approve our test account." **Manager:** "How long do you think that will take?" **Developer:** "They said 3-5 business days, so we should be back on track by next week."

3. Discussing Deadlines and Timelines

These phrases help you talk about time constraints realistically and manage expectations.

Expression: "The deadline is tight, but doable."

- **Explanation:** A balanced way to acknowledge time pressure while expressing confidence that the goal can be achieved.

- **Example:** "The client wants this by Friday. **The deadline is tight, but doable** if we focus on the core features first."

Expression: "We're cutting it close."

- **Explanation:** An honest way to say that timing will be very tight and there's little room for delays or problems.

- **Example:** "**We're cutting it close** with the presentation deadline. We need everything finalized by tomorrow morning."

Expression: "We need to push back the deadline."

- **Explanation:** A direct way to communicate that a deadline cannot be met and needs to be extended. It's better to communicate this early than to miss the deadline.

- **Example:** "Given the scope changes, **we need to push back the deadline** by one week to ensure quality."

Expression: "If we stick to the timeline..."

- **Explanation:** A way to discuss what will happen if the current schedule is maintained. Often used to set expectations or highlight dependencies.

- **Example:** "**If we stick to the timeline**, we'll have the prototype ready for user testing next month."

4. Collaborative Problem-Solving

These expressions help teams work together to overcome challenges and find solutions.

Expression: "Let's put our heads together."

- **Explanation:** An encouraging phrase that invites collaborative thinking and problem-solving. It suggests that combined effort will find a solution.

- **Example:** "This is a complex issue. **Let's put our heads together** and see if we can find a creative solution."

Expression: "What's our best option here?"

- **Explanation:** A question that focuses the team on finding practical solutions rather than dwelling on problems.

- **Example:** "The original plan isn't working. **What's our best option here?** Should we try a different approach?"

Expression: "Let's brainstorm some alternatives."

- **Explanation:** A structured way to invite creative thinking and generate multiple potential solutions to a problem.

- **Example:** "The budget for the original design is too high. **Let's brainstorm some alternatives** that could achieve the same goals for less money."

Expression: "We need a workaround."

- **Explanation:** A practical phrase used when the ideal solution isn't available and you need to find an alternative way to achieve the goal.

- **Example:** "The software we planned to use isn't available until next month. **We need a workaround** to keep the project moving."

Scenario: Problem-Solving Session

Team Lead: "The client just told us they need the project delivered two weeks earlier than planned." **Designer:** "That's going to be challenging. **What's our best option here?**" **Team Lead:** "**Let's put our heads together.** What if we delivered the core features first and added the nice-to-have features in a second phase?" **Developer:** "That could work. **Let's brainstorm some alternatives** for which features are truly essential." **Designer:** "Good idea. We might **need a workaround** for the custom animations - maybe we use standard ones for now."

Common Mistakes and How to Avoid Them

Mistake 1: Being Vague About Responsibilities. Saying "someone should handle this" or "we need to work on that" doesn't clearly assign ownership.

- **How to Avoid:** Always be specific about who is responsible for what. Use names and clear action items: "Sarah, could you take the lead on the market research by Friday?"

Mistake 2: Hiding Problems Until It's Too Late. Waiting until a deadline is missed to report issues can damage trust and make problems harder to solve.

- **How to Avoid:** Report problems early using phrases like "We've hit a snag with..." This gives the team time to find solutions.

Mistake 3: Making Unrealistic Commitments. Agreeing to impossible deadlines to please stakeholders often leads to poor quality work or missed deadlines.

- **How to Avoid:** Be honest about what's achievable. Use phrases like "The deadline is tight, but doable" only when it's truly realistic.

Try This: Your Turn to Practice

Scenario: You're managing a project to launch a new company website. The graphic designer just told you that creating the custom illustrations will take two weeks longer than originally planned. This puts your launch date at risk. You need to update your team and find a solution.

Your Task:

1. How would you report this problem to your team using one of the phrases from this chapter?

2. How would you invite the team to work together to find a solution?

3. What might be a potential workaround you could suggest?

(Practice your responses. For example: "We've hit a snag with the custom illustrations - they'll take two weeks longer than planned. Let's put our heads together to find a solution. What if we used stock illustrations for the launch and added custom ones in a later update?")

Chapter 5: Key Takeaways

Delegate Clearly: Use phrases like "Could you take the lead on..." and "I'd like you to handle..." to assign responsibilities clearly and respectfully.

Report Honestly: Keep stakeholders informed with phrases like "We're on track to..." and "We've hit a snag with..." to maintain trust and enable good decision-making.

Manage Expectations: Be realistic about deadlines using phrases like "The deadline is tight, but doable" and communicate early if you "need to push back the deadline."

Solve Problems Together: Use collaborative language like "Let's put our heads together" and "What's our best option here?" to engage your team in finding solutions.

CHAPTER FIVE

Navigating Difficult Conversations and Constructive Feedback

Some of the most important conversations in business are also the most challenging ones. Whether you need to deliver constructive feedback to a colleague, decline a request from your boss, address a performance issue, or de-escalate a tense situation, how you handle these difficult moments can define your professional relationships and career trajectory. Many professionals avoid these conversations altogether, which often makes problems worse. Others approach them too directly and create unnecessary conflict. This chapter provides you with the essential phrases and expressions to navigate sensitive topics with confidence, professionalism, and tact. You will learn how to give and receive feedback constructively, say "no" diplomatically, and turn potentially confrontational situations into productive discussions.

Essential Expressions for Difficult Conversations

Here are the key phrases for handling sensitive workplace situations with professionalism and grace. Each is explained with a simple definition and a realistic usage example.

1. Giving Constructive Feedback

These phrases help you deliver feedback in a way that motivates improvement rather than creating defensiveness.

Expression: "I've noticed that..." / "I've observed that..."

- **Explanation:** A neutral, factual way to begin feedback. It focuses on specific behaviors rather than making personal judgments.

- **Example:** "**I've noticed that** the last few reports have been submitted after the deadline. Can we talk about what might be causing this?"

Expression: "I'd like to see..." / "It would be great if..."

- **Explanation:** A positive way to suggest improvements by focusing on desired outcomes rather than criticizing current performance.

- **Example:** "**I'd like to see** more detailed analysis in your presentations. **It would be great if** you could include more supporting data."

Expression: "Moving forward..."

- **Explanation:** A phrase that shifts the conversation from past problems to future solutions. It's forward-looking and constructive.

- **Example:** "I understand there were some challenges with the last project. **Moving forward**, let's establish clearer checkpoints to catch issues early."

Scenario: Performance Review

Manager: "Overall, your work quality is excellent, but **I've noticed that** you sometimes miss our team meetings." **Employee:** "Oh, I didn't realize it was that noticeable. I've been swamped with the Johnson project." **Manager:** "I understand you're busy, and your dedication is appreciated. **Moving forward, it would be great if** you could let me know in advance when you can't make a meeting." **Employee:** "Absolutely. I'll make sure to communicate better."

2. Receiving Feedback Gracefully

These expressions help you respond to criticism professionally and show you're open to improvement.

Expression: "I appreciate the feedback."

- **Explanation:** A professional way to acknowledge feedback, even if it's difficult to hear. It shows maturity and openness to growth.

- **Example:** "**I appreciate the feedback.** I wasn't aware that my communication style was coming across as too direct."

Expression: "You're absolutely right."

- **Explanation:** A straightforward way to accept valid criticism. It shows accountability and prevents defensive arguments.

- **Example:** "**You're absolutely right.** I should have consulted with the team before making that decision."

Expression: "How can I improve this?"

- **Explanation:** A proactive question that shows you're committed to getting better. It turns criticism into a learning opportunity.

- **Example:** "I see what you mean about the presentation being unclear. **How can I improve this** for next time?"

3. Politely Declining Requests

These phrases help you say "no" professionally without damaging relationships.

Expression: "I'm afraid I don't have the bandwidth right now."

- **Explanation:** A professional way to decline a request due to workload. "Bandwidth" is a business term for available capacity or time.

- **Example:** "That sounds like an interesting project, but **I'm afraid I don't have the bandwidth right now** with the quarterly reports due."

Expression: "I wish I could help, but..."

- **Explanation:** A sympathetic way to decline that shows you genuinely want to help but have legitimate constraints.

- **Example:** "**I wish I could help, but** I'm committed to the marketing campaign until the end of the month."

Expression: "That's outside my area of expertise."

- **Explanation:** A honest way to decline when you're not the right person for the task. It's better than accepting something you can't do well.

- **Example:** "**That's outside my area of expertise.** You might want to check with someone from the IT department."

Scenario: Declining Additional Work

Colleague: "Hey, Sarah, could you help me with the budget analysis for the new project? I'm really struggling with it." **Sarah:** "**I wish I could help, but** I'm completely swamped with the client presentation that's due tomorrow." **Colleague:** "Oh, I understand. When do you think you might have some time?" **Sarah:** "Honestly, **I'm afraid I don't have the bandwidth** until after the presentation. But have you tried asking Mike? He's really good with financial analysis."

4. De-escalating Conflict

These expressions help you calm tense situations and redirect conversations toward solutions.

Expression: "I can see your point of view."

- **Explanation:** A powerful phrase for acknowledging someone's perspective without necessarily agreeing with it. It helps reduce defensiveness.

- **Example:** "**I can see your point of view** about the timeline being too aggressive. Let's look at what's realistic."

Expression: "Let's take a step back."

- **Explanation:** A way to pause a heated discussion and refocus on the bigger picture or core issues.

- **Example:** "We're getting caught up in the details. **Let's take a step back** and remember what we're trying to achieve here."

Expression: "I understand your frustration."

- **Explanation:** An empathetic response that validates someone's emotions without taking blame. It helps defuse anger and opens the door to problem-solving.

- **Example:** "**I understand your frustration** with the delays. Let's figure out how to get this back on track."

Expression: "Let's find a solution that works for everyone."

- **Explanation:** A collaborative phrase that shifts focus from blame to problem-solving and emphasizes mutual benefit.

- **Example:** "We clearly have different priorities here. **Let's find a solution that works for everyone.**"

Scenario: Resolving a Team Conflict

Team Member A: "This is ridiculous! We keep changing the requirements every week. How are we supposed to get anything done?" **Project Manager: "I understand your frustration.** The constant changes are definitely challenging." **Team Member A:** "It's not just challenging, it's impossible!" **Project Manager: "I can see your point of view. Let's take a step back** and look at which requirements are truly essential and which ones we can postpone." **Team Member B:** "That sounds reasonable. I'm tired of redoing work too." **Project Manager:** "Great. **Let's find a solution that works for everyone.** How about we freeze the requirements for the next two weeks?"

Common Mistakes and How to Avoid Them

Mistake 1: Making It Personal. Using "you always" or "you never" statements makes people defensive and shifts focus from behavior to character.

- **How to Avoid:** Focus on specific behaviors and situations. Say "I've noticed that the last three reports were late" instead of "You're always late with reports."

Mistake 2: Avoiding Difficult Conversations. Hoping problems will resolve themselves usually makes them worse and can damage your credibility as a leader.

- **How to Avoid:** Address issues early using gentle phrases like "I've observed that..." The longer you wait, the harder the conversation becomes.

Mistake 3: Being Too Blunt When Declining. Simply saying "No, I can't" without explanation can seem rude and unhelpful.

- **How to Avoid:** Always provide a brief reason and, when possible, suggest alternatives: "I'm afraid I don't have the bandwidth, but you might try asking..."

Try This: Your Turn to Practice

Scenario 1: A colleague consistently interrupts you and others during team meetings. It's becoming disruptive and affecting team morale. You want to address this with them privately.

Your Task: How would you start this conversation using the feedback phrases from this chapter?

Scenario 2: Your manager asks you to take on a major project that would require working weekends for the next month. You already have a full workload and personal commitments.

Your Task: How would you politely decline this request while maintaining a good relationship with your manager?

(Practice your responses. For example, Scenario 1: "Hi John, I wanted to chat with you about something. I've noticed that during our team meetings, there's been a lot of interrupting happening. Moving forward, it would be great if we could let people finish their thoughts before jumping in." Scenario 2: "I appreciate you thinking of me for this project. I wish I could help, but I'm afraid I don't have the bandwidth to give it the attention it deserves with my current workload.")

Chapter 6: Key Takeaways

Give Feedback Constructively: Use "I've noticed that..." and "Moving forward..." to focus on specific behaviors and future improvements rather than personal criticism.

Receive Feedback Gracefully: Respond with "I appreciate the feedback" and "How can I improve this?" to show professionalism and commitment to growth.

Decline Diplomatically: Use phrases like "I'm afraid I don't have the bandwidth" and "I wish I could help, but..." to say no while maintaining relationships.

De-escalate Conflicts: Acknowledge perspectives with "I can see your point of view" and redirect to solutions with "Let's find a solution that works for everyone."

CHAPTER SIX

Winning Job Interviews

Job interviews are high-stakes conversations where every word matters. In the span of 30 to 60 minutes, you need to convince strangers that you're the right person for the job, demonstrate your expertise, show your personality, and prove you'll fit well with their team culture. The pressure can be intense, but the right language can transform your interview from a nerve-wracking interrogation into a confident, engaging conversation. This chapter provides you with the essential phrases and expressions that will help you shine in any interview setting. You will learn how to make a powerful first impression, answer challenging questions with confidence, ask thoughtful questions that demonstrate your interest and expertise, and leave interviewers with a lasting positive impression.

Essential Expressions for Job Interviews

Here are the key phrases for every stage of the interview process, from the opening handshake to the closing follow-up. Each is explained with a simple definition and a realistic usage example.

1. Making a Strong First Impression

The first few minutes of an interview set the tone for everything that follows. These phrases help you start confidently.

Expression: "Thank you for taking the time to meet with me today."

- **Explanation:** A professional and gracious opening that acknowledges the interviewer's time and shows appreciation for the opportunity.

- **Example:** "Good morning, Ms. Johnson. **Thank you for taking the time to meet with me today.** I'm really excited to learn more about this opportunity."

Expression: "I'm thrilled to be here."

- **Explanation:** Shows genuine enthusiasm for the opportunity without sounding overly casual. "Thrilled" is more professional than "excited."

- **Example:** "**I'm thrilled to be here.** When I saw this position posted, I knew it was exactly what I was looking for in my next role."

Expression: "I've been looking forward to this conversation."

- **Explanation:** Frames the interview as a mutual discussion rather than a one-sided evaluation. It shows you're engaged and prepared.

- **Example:** "**I've been looking forward to this conversation.**

I've done quite a bit of research on your company, and I'm impressed by your recent expansion into the European market."

2. Answering Key Interview Questions

These phrases help you structure your responses to common interview questions in a compelling way.

Expression: "In my previous role..." / "In my experience..."

- **Explanation:** A strong way to begin examples that demonstrate your relevant experience and achievements.

- **Example:** "**In my previous role** as marketing manager, I led a campaign that increased customer engagement by 40% in just six months."

Expression: "What I found particularly rewarding was..."

- **Explanation:** A way to highlight achievements while showing what motivates you. It demonstrates both competence and passion.

- **Example:** "**What I found particularly rewarding was** mentoring junior team members and seeing them develop their skills and confidence."

Expression: "I'm particularly proud of..."

- **Explanation:** A confident way to highlight your best

achievements without sounding boastful. It shows you take ownership of your successes.

- **Example:** "I'm particularly proud of the customer retention program I developed, which reduced churn by 25% and saved the company over $200,000 annually."

Expression: "That's a great question. Let me think about that for a moment."

- **Explanation:** Buys you time to formulate a thoughtful response to unexpected or complex questions. It shows you take the question seriously.

- **Example:** (When asked about handling a difficult situation) "**That's a great question. Let me think about that for a moment.** I believe the key is to stay calm and focus on finding solutions rather than assigning blame."

Scenario: Behavioral Interview Question

Interviewer: "Tell me about a time when you had to deal with a difficult team member." **Candidate:** "**That's a great question. In my previous role** as project manager, I worked with someone who consistently missed deadlines and didn't communicate well with the rest of the team." **Interviewer:** "How did you handle that?" **Candidate:** "I scheduled a private conversation to understand what was causing the issues. It turned out they were overwhelmed and didn't know how to ask for help. **What I found particularly rewarding was** being able to provide the support they needed and seeing them become one of our most reliable team members."

3. Asking Insightful Questions

Asking good questions shows you're serious about the role and helps you evaluate if the company is right for you.

Expression: "I'm curious about..."

- **Explanation:** A natural way to introduce questions that shows genuine interest and engagement with the role or company.

- **Example: "I'm curious about** the team dynamics. How does the marketing team collaborate with sales and product development?"

Expression: "What does success look like in this role?"

- **Explanation:** A strategic question that helps you understand expectations and shows you're focused on delivering results.

- **Example: "What does success look like in this role** after the first six months? What would you expect me to have accomplished?"

Expression: "What are the biggest challenges facing the team right now?"

- **Explanation:** Shows you're thinking strategically about how you can contribute and that you're not afraid of challenges.

- **Example: "What are the biggest challenges facing the team right now?** I'd love to understand where I could make the most immediate impact."

Expression: "How would you describe the company culture?"

- **Explanation:** An important question for determining fit. It shows you care about more than just the job duties.

- **Example: "How would you describe the company culture?** What type of person tends to thrive here?"

4. Demonstrating Interest and Enthusiasm

These phrases help you show genuine interest in the role and company throughout the interview.

Expression: "That aligns perfectly with my experience in..."

- **Explanation:** A way to connect your background directly to what they're looking for. It shows you're listening and making relevant connections.

- **Example: "That aligns perfectly with my experience in** digital marketing. I've worked extensively with social media campaigns and data analytics."

Expression: "I'd love the opportunity to..."

- **Explanation:** Shows enthusiasm for specific aspects of the role and demonstrates forward-thinking about your potential contributions.

- **Example:** "**I'd love the opportunity to** bring my experience with international markets to help expand your presence in Asia."

Expression: "Based on what you've told me..."

- **Explanation:** Shows you've been actively listening and can synthesize information. It demonstrates engagement and analytical thinking.

- **Example:** "**Based on what you've told me** about the company's growth plans, it sounds like this role will be crucial for scaling the operations team."

Scenario: Showing Interest and Fit

Interviewer: "We're looking for someone who can manage multiple projects simultaneously while maintaining attention to detail." **Candidate:** "**That aligns perfectly with my experience** as operations coordinator. **In my previous role**, I managed up to eight client projects at once while maintaining a 99% accuracy rate on deliverables." **Interviewer:** "That's impressive. What interests you most about this particular role?" **Candidate:** "**I'd love the opportunity to** apply my project management skills in a larger organization. **Based on what**

you've told me about your expansion plans, it sounds like there will be exciting challenges ahead."

Common Mistakes and How to Avoid Them

Mistake 1: Speaking Negatively About Previous Employers. Criticizing former bosses or companies makes you look unprofessional and raises red flags about your attitude.

- **How to Avoid:** Focus on what you learned and what you're looking for next. Instead of "My boss was terrible," say "I'm looking for an environment where I can have more autonomy and growth opportunities."

Mistake 2: Not Preparing Questions. Saying "I don't have any questions" suggests you're not genuinely interested in the role or company.

- **How to Avoid:** Always prepare 3-5 thoughtful questions about the role, team, company culture, and growth opportunities. Write them down if necessary.

Mistake 3: Being Too Modest. Downplaying your achievements or saying "it was a team effort" without highlighting your specific contributions can make you seem unconfident.

- **How to Avoid:** Use phrases like "I'm particularly proud of..." and be specific about your contributions while still acknowledging team collaboration.

Try This: Your Turn to Practice

Scenario: You're interviewing for a marketing manager position at a growing tech startup. The interviewer asks: "Why are you interested in leaving your current job to join a startup?"

Your Task:

1. How would you frame your response positively without criticizing your current employer?

2. What question could you ask to show your interest in the startup environment?

3. How would you connect your experience to what they might need?

(Practice your responses. For example: "In my current role, I've learned a tremendous amount about marketing strategy, but I'm looking for an environment where I can have more direct impact on business growth. That aligns perfectly with my experience in launching new products. I'm curious about what the biggest marketing challenges are for the company right now?")

Chapter 7: Key Takeaways

Start Strong: Open with appreciation using "Thank you for taking the time to meet with me" and show enthusiasm with "I'm thrilled to be here."

Answer with Examples: Use "In my previous role..." and "I'm particularly proud of..." to provide concrete evidence of your capabilities.

Ask Strategic Questions: Show genuine interest with "I'm curious about..." and "What does success look like in this role?" to demonstrate engagement.

Stay Positive: Focus on what you're looking for rather than what you're trying to escape, and always highlight your specific contributions to team successes.

CHAPTER SEVEN

Networking Like a Pro

Networking is one of the most powerful tools for career advancement, business development, and professional growth. Yet many people approach networking events with dread, unsure of how to start conversations with strangers, make meaningful connections, or follow up effectively. The secret to successful networking isn't about collecting as many business cards as possible—it's about building genuine relationships through authentic conversations and mutual value exchange. This chapter provides you with the essential phrases and expressions that will transform you from an awkward networker into a confident relationship builder. You will learn how to approach new contacts naturally, introduce yourself in a memorable way, engage in meaningful conversations, and maintain relationships that benefit everyone involved.

Essential Expressions for Professional Networking

Here are the key phrases for every aspect of networking, from initial introductions to long-term relationship maintenance. Each is explained with a simple definition and a realistic usage example.

1. Approaching New Contacts

These phrases help you start conversations naturally and confidently at networking events or professional gatherings.

Expression: "Excuse me, I don't think we've met."

- **Explanation:** A polite and professional way to introduce yourself to someone new. It's direct but friendly and opens the door for introductions.

- **Example:** "**Excuse me, I don't think we've met.** I'm Sarah Chen from Digital Marketing Solutions."

Expression: "I couldn't help but overhear..."

- **Explanation:** A natural way to join a conversation that's already in progress, especially when you have something relevant to contribute.

- **Example:** "**I couldn't help but overhear** you talking about the challenges with remote team management. I've been dealing with similar issues."

Expression: "Are you enjoying the event?"

- **Explanation:** A safe, neutral conversation starter that works in any networking situation. It's open-ended and gives the other person a chance to share their experience.

- **Example:** "Hi there! **Are you enjoying the event?** This is my first time at this conference, and I'm impressed by the speaker lineup."

2. Memorable Self-Introductions

These phrases help you introduce yourself in a way that people will remember and want to continue talking with.

Expression: "I help [target audience] [achieve specific result]."

- **Explanation:** A clear, benefit-focused way to describe what you do that's more engaging than just stating your job title.
- **Example:** "**I help small businesses** streamline their accounting processes so they can focus on growing their revenue."

Expression: "I work with [industry/type of client] to [solve specific problem]."

- **Explanation:** Another variation that focuses on the value you provide rather than just your role or company name.
- **Example:** "**I work with tech startups to** develop marketing strategies that help them reach their target customers more effectively."

Expression: "What brings you to [event/conference]?"

- **Explanation:** A great follow-up question after introductions that shows interest in the other person and often leads to meaningful conversation.

- **Example:** "Nice to meet you, David. **What brings you to** the Digital Marketing Summit? Are you looking to learn about any particular topics?"

Scenario: Conference Networking

Alex: "**Excuse me, I don't think we've met.** I'm Alex Rodriguez." **Maria:** "Hi Alex, I'm Maria Santos. Nice to meet you." **Alex:** "Likewise. **What brings you to** the conference today?" **Maria:** "I'm here to learn about the latest trends in customer experience. I'm a CX manager at TechFlow." **Alex:** "That's interesting. **I help companies** improve their customer onboarding processes. There might be some overlap in what we do."

3. Building Meaningful Connections

These expressions help you move beyond small talk to create genuine professional relationships.

Expression: "That's fascinating. Tell me more about..."

- **Explanation:** Shows genuine interest in what the other person does and encourages them to share more details. People appreciate when others are truly interested in their work.

- **Example:** "**That's fascinating. Tell me more about** how you're using AI in your customer service operations."

Expression: "I'd love to learn more about your experience with..."

- **Explanation:** A way to show respect for someone's expertise while potentially learning something valuable for your own work.

- **Example:** "I'd love to learn more about your experience **with** international expansion. We're considering entering the European market."

Expression: "Have you found any effective strategies for...?"

- **Explanation:** A collaborative question that positions you as someone seeking to learn and improve. It often leads to valuable insights and mutual problem-solving.

- **Example: "Have you found any effective strategies for** retaining top talent in this competitive market?"

Expression: "I might be able to help with that."

- **Explanation:** A generous offer that shows you're thinking about how you can provide value to the other person, not just what you can get from them.

- **Example:** "You mentioned struggling with social media engagement. **I might be able to help with that**—it's actually one of my specialties."

4. Following Up and Maintaining Relationships

These phrases help you stay connected with your network and build lasting professional relationships.

Expression: "It was great meeting you at [event]."

- **Explanation:** A warm way to begin a follow-up message that reminds the person where you met and reinforces the positive connection.

- **Example:** "Hi David, **it was great meeting you at** the Marketing Summit last week. I really enjoyed our conversation about customer retention strategies."

Expression: "I thought you might find this interesting..."

- **Explanation:** A valuable way to stay in touch by sharing relevant articles, opportunities, or insights that could benefit your contact.

- **Example:** "**I thought you might find this interesting**—I came across an article about new developments in AI customer service that relates to what we discussed."

Expression: "I'd love to continue our conversation over coffee."

- **Explanation:** A natural way to suggest a follow-up meeting that feels casual and non-threatening while showing genuine interest in building the relationship.

- **Example:** "**I'd love to continue our conversation over coffee.**

Would you be available for a brief chat sometime next week?"

Expression: "Please don't hesitate to reach out if..."

- **Explanation:** A generous closing that leaves the door open for future collaboration and shows you're willing to help when needed.

- **Example:** "Please don't hesitate to reach out if you have any questions about digital marketing strategies. I'm always happy to share insights."

Scenario: Follow-up Email

Subject: Great meeting you at the Tech Conference

Hi Jennifer,

It was great meeting you at the Tech Innovation Conference yesterday. I really enjoyed our discussion about the challenges of scaling customer support operations.

I thought you might find this interesting—I came across a case study about how a similar company reduced support tickets by 40% using chatbot automation. I've attached the link below.

I'd love to continue our conversation over coffee if you're interested. I think there might be some opportunities for our companies to collaborate.

Please don't hesitate to reach out if you have any questions about marketing automation. I'm always happy to share what I've learned.

Best regards, Michael

Common Mistakes and How to Avoid Them

Mistake 1: Leading with a Sales Pitch. Immediately trying to sell your services or products makes people uncomfortable and damages potential relationships.

- **How to Avoid:** Focus on building genuine connections first. Ask questions about their business and challenges before mentioning how you might help.

Mistake 2: Collecting Cards Without Building Relationships. Gathering business cards without having meaningful conversations is a waste of time for everyone involved.

- **How to Avoid:** Aim for quality over quantity. Have fewer, deeper conversations rather than rushing through superficial introductions.

Mistake 3: Failing to Follow Up. Meeting someone and never contacting them again means you've wasted the networking opportunity.

- **How to Avoid:** Send a follow-up message within 48 hours of meeting someone. Reference your conversation and suggest a specific next step.

Try This: Your Turn to Practice

Scenario: You're at an industry conference and notice someone standing alone near the refreshment table. They're wearing a name tag that shows they work for a company you've heard good things about.

Your Task:

1. How would you approach this person and start a conversation?

2. How would you introduce yourself in a memorable way?

3. What questions could you ask to learn more about their work and build a connection?

(Practice your responses. For example: "Excuse me, I don't think we've met. I'm [Your Name]. Are you enjoying the conference?" followed by "I help [description of what you do]. What brings you to the conference today?" and then "That's fascinating. Tell me more about what you're working on at [Company Name].")

Chapter 8: Key Takeaways

Approach Naturally: Use phrases like "Excuse me, I don't think we've met" and "Are you enjoying the event?" to start conversations comfortably.

Introduce with Value: Describe what you do in terms of how you help people rather than just stating your job title.

Show Genuine Interest: Use "That's fascinating. Tell me more about..." and "I'd love to learn more about your experience with..." to build meaningful connections.

Follow Up Consistently: Always follow up within 48 hours using "It was great meeting you at..." and provide value with "I thought you might find this interesting..."

CHAPTER EIGHT

Public Speaking and Powerful Presentations

Public speaking is one of the most feared activities in the professional world, yet it's also one of the most powerful tools for career advancement. Whether you're presenting quarterly results to your team, pitching a new idea to executives, or speaking at an industry conference, your ability to communicate clearly and confidently in front of an audience can set you apart as a leader and subject matter expert. The difference between a forgettable presentation and a memorable one often comes down to the specific words and phrases you use to structure your message, engage your audience, and handle unexpected situations. This chapter provides you with the essential expressions that will transform your presentations from nervous stumbles into confident, compelling communications that inspire action and leave lasting impressions.

Essential Expressions for Public Speaking

Here are the key phrases for every aspect of presenting, from opening hooks to closing calls-to-action. Each is explained with a simple definition and a realistic usage example.

1. Engaging Openings

The first few minutes of your presentation are crucial for capturing attention and setting expectations. These phrases help you start strong.

Expression: "Thank you all for being here today."

- **Explanation:** A warm, appreciative opening that acknowledges your audience's time and creates a positive atmosphere from the start.

- **Example: "Thank you all for being here today.** I know how busy everyone is, so I appreciate you taking the time to join me for this important discussion."

Expression: "I'm excited to share with you..."

Explanation: Shows enthusiasm for your topic and creates anticipation for what's coming. Enthusiasm is contagious and helps engage your audience.

Example: "I'm excited to share with you the results of our customer satisfaction survey and what they mean for our product development strategy."

Expression: "By the end of this presentation, you'll..."

- **Explanation:** Sets clear expectations and tells your audience what value they'll receive. It gives them a reason to pay attention.

- **Example:** "**By the end of this presentation, you'll** understand our new marketing strategy and know exactly how it will impact your department."

Expression: "Let me start with a question..."

- **Explanation:** An interactive way to begin that immediately engages your audience and gets them thinking about your topic.

- **Example:** "**Let me start with a question:** How many of you have experienced frustration with our current project management system? I see quite a few hands."

2. Clear Transitions and Structure

These phrases help your audience follow your logic and understand how different parts of your presentation connect.

Expression: "Now that we've covered..., let's move on to..."

- **Explanation:** A clear transition that summarizes what you've just discussed and previews what's coming next. It helps maintain flow and clarity.

- **Example:** "**Now that we've covered** the current market challenges, **let's move on to** our proposed solutions."

Expression: "This brings me to my next point..."

- **Explanation:** A smooth way to transition between ideas that shows logical progression and keeps your audience engaged.

- **Example:** "As you can see, customer retention has improved significantly. **This brings me to my next point** about how we can build on this success."

Expression: "To put this in perspective..."

- **Explanation:** Helps your audience understand the significance or context of the information you're presenting.

- **Example:** "We've reduced processing time by 30 seconds per transaction. **To put this in perspective**, that saves us over 200 hours of work per month."

Expression: "The key takeaway here is..."

- **Explanation:** Highlights the most important point from a section, ensuring your audience doesn't miss critical information.

- **Example:** "We've looked at several different approaches to this problem. **The key takeaway here is** that automation will give us the biggest return on investment."

3. Maintaining Audience Engagement

These phrases help you keep your audience interested and involved throughout your presentation.

Expression: "As you can see on this slide..."

- **Explanation:** Directs attention to visual elements and helps integrate your slides with your spoken content.

- **Example:** "**As you can see on this slide**, our sales have increased by 25% in each of the last three quarters."

Expression: "This is particularly important because..."

- **Explanation:** Emphasizes significance and helps your audience understand why they should care about a particular point.

- **Example:** "**This is particularly important because** it affects not just our department, but the entire customer experience."

Expression: "Let me give you a concrete example..."

- **Explanation:** Introduces real-world examples that make abstract concepts more relatable and memorable.

- **Example:** "**Let me give you a concrete example** of how this new process worked for our biggest client."

Expression: "I want to emphasize that..."

- **Explanation:** Draws attention to critical points and ensures your audience remembers the most important information.

- **Example:** "**I want to emphasize that** this change will require everyone's cooperation to be successful."

4. Handling Questions and Interaction

These phrases help you manage audience questions professionally and maintain control of your presentation.

Expression: "That's an excellent question."

- **Explanation:** A positive response that validates the questioner and gives you a moment to think about your answer.

- **Example:** "**That's an excellent question.** The implementation timeline will depend on several factors, including budget approval and resource availability."

Expression: "I'm glad you brought that up."

- **Explanation:** Shows appreciation for the question and suggests it's relevant to your presentation topic.

- **Example:** "**I'm glad you brought that up.** Security is indeed a major consideration, and I have a slide that addresses exactly that concern."

Expression: "Let me address that in two parts..."

- **Explanation:** A way to organize complex answers and ensure you cover all aspects of a multi-faceted question.

- **Example:** "**Let me address that in two parts:** first, the technical requirements, and second, the training implications."

Expression: "I'll come back to that at the end."

- **Explanation:** A diplomatic way to defer questions that you plan to address later in your presentation, maintaining your planned flow.

- **Example:** "**I'll come back to that at the end** when we discuss implementation timelines. I have detailed information on that topic."

5. Strong Closings and Calls to Action

These phrases help you end your presentation memorably and motivate your audience to take action.

Expression: "To summarize the key points..."

- **Explanation:** Signals that you're wrapping up and helps reinforce your main messages one final time.

- **Example:** "**To summarize the key points:** we've identified the problem, explored three potential solutions, and recommended the most cost-effective approach."

Expression: "The next steps are..."

- **Explanation:** Provides clear direction for what should happen after your presentation, turning ideas into action.

- **Example: "The next steps are** to get budget approval by Friday, form the implementation team next week, and begin the pilot program by month-end."

Expression: "I encourage you to..."

- **Explanation:** A motivational way to suggest specific actions your audience should take based on your presentation.

- **Example: "I encourage you to** think about how these strategies could apply to your own projects and reach out if you'd like to discuss implementation."

Expression: "Thank you for your attention. I'm happy to take any questions."

- **Explanation:** A professional closing that shows appreciation and opens the floor for discussion.

- **Example: "Thank you for your attention. I'm happy to take any questions** about the proposal or the implementation process."

Scenario: Quarterly Business Review Presentation

Presenter: "**Thank you all for being here today. I'm excited to share with you** our Q3 results and our strategy for Q4."

(After covering the results)

Presenter: "**As you can see on this slide**, we exceeded our revenue targets by 15%. **This is particularly important because** it positions us well for our year-end goals."

(During Q&A)

Audience Member: "What about the challenges in the European market?" **Presenter:** "**That's an excellent question. Let me address that in two parts:** the regulatory challenges and the competitive landscape."

(Closing)

Presenter: "**To summarize the key points:** we've had a strong Q3, identified areas for improvement, and outlined our Q4 strategy. **The next steps are** to finalize our budget allocations and begin implementation next week. **Thank you for your attention. I'm happy to take any questions.**"

Common Mistakes and How to Avoid Them

Mistake 1: Reading Directly from Slides. Simply reading your slides word-for-word makes you seem unprepared and bores your audience.

- **How to Avoid:** Use slides as visual support, not a script. Practice speaking about each slide using phrases like "As you can see..." to integrate visuals with your narrative.

Mistake 2: Ignoring Time Limits. Running over your allotted time shows disrespect for your audience's schedule and can undermine your message.

- **How to Avoid:** Practice your presentation multiple times and build in buffer time. Use phrases like "To summarize..." to wrap up efficiently if you're running short on time.

Mistake 3: Avoiding Eye Contact. Looking at the floor, ceiling, or only at your slides makes you seem nervous and disconnected from your audience.

- **How to Avoid:** Practice making eye contact with different sections of your audience. When using phrases like "Let me give you a concrete example," look directly at your audience to create connection.

Try This: Your Turn to Practice

Scenario: You need to present a proposal for a new employee training program to your company's leadership team. You have 15 minutes to present and 5 minutes for questions.

Your Task:

1. How would you open your presentation to capture attention and set expectations?

2. How would you transition from explaining the problem to

presenting your solution?

3. How would you close with a clear call to action?

(Practice your responses. For example: Opening: "Thank you all for being here today. I'm excited to share with you a proposal that could improve employee retention by 30%. By the end of this presentation, you'll understand the current training gaps and see exactly how we can address them." Transition: "Now that we've covered the challenges our employees are facing, let's move on to the solution I'm proposing." Closing: "To summarize the key points: we have a training gap, this program addresses it cost-effectively, and implementation can begin next month. The next steps are to approve the budget and select the pilot group. I encourage you to consider the long-term benefits of investing in our people.")

Chapter 9: Key Takeaways

Start Strong: Use "Thank you all for being here today" and "I'm excited to share with you..." to create a positive, engaging opening.

Guide Your Audience: Use clear transitions like "Now that we've covered..." and "This brings me to my next point..." to maintain logical flow.

Engage Throughout: Keep attention with phrases like "As you can see on this slide..." and "Let me give you a concrete example..."

Handle Questions Professionally: Respond with "That's an excellent question" and "I'm glad you brought that up" to maintain positive interaction.

End with Action: Close strong using "To summarize the key points..." and "The next steps are..." to drive results from your presentation.

CHAPTER NINE

Leading with Impactful Language

Leadership is fundamentally about communication. The words you choose as a leader don't just convey information—they shape culture, inspire action, build confidence, and drive results. Whether you're managing a small team or leading an entire organization, your language has the power to motivate people to achieve extraordinary things or to demoralize them into mediocrity. Great leaders understand that how they communicate is just as important as what they communicate. This chapter provides you with the essential phrases and expressions that distinguish exceptional leaders from average managers. You will learn how to motivate and inspire your team, delegate effectively while maintaining accountability, provide direction during uncertainty, and create a culture of excellence through the power of your words.

Essential Expressions for Leadership Communication

Here are the key phrases that effective leaders use to inspire, motivate, and guide their teams toward success. Each is explained with a simple definition and a realistic usage example.

1. Motivating and Inspiring Teams

These phrases help you energize your team and create enthusiasm for challenging goals and projects.

Expression: "I have complete confidence in this team."

- **Explanation:** A powerful statement that builds team confidence and shows your trust in their abilities. It creates a positive expectation of success.

- **Example:** "This is an ambitious project, but **I have complete confidence in this team.** We have the skills and experience to make this happen."

Expression: "We're going to make a real difference here."

- **Explanation:** Connects the team's work to a larger purpose and meaning, which is one of the strongest motivators for high performance.

- **Example:** "This new customer service initiative isn't just about improving metrics. **We're going to make a real difference** in how our customers experience our brand."

Expression: "This is our opportunity to..."

- **Explanation:** Frames challenges as opportunities and helps the team see the positive potential in difficult situations.

- **Example:** "The market downturn is challenging, but **this is our opportunity to** gain market share while our competitors are struggling."

Expression: "I believe in what we're doing here."

- **Explanation:** Shows personal commitment and conviction, which inspires others to share your enthusiasm and dedication.

- **Example:** "**I believe in what we're doing here.** This product has the potential to transform how people manage their finances."

2. Delegating with Clarity and Empowerment

These phrases help you assign responsibilities in a way that empowers your team while ensuring accountability.

Expression: "I'm counting on you to..."

- **Explanation:** Shows trust and creates a sense of personal responsibility. It's more empowering than simply giving orders.

- **Example:** "Sarah, **I'm counting on you to** lead the client presentation next week. You know their business better than anyone."

Expression: "You have my full support on this."

- **Explanation:** Assures team members that you'll back them up and provide resources they need to succeed.

- **Example:** "This is a challenging project, but **you have my full support.** If you need additional resources or help removing obstacles, just let me know."

Expression: "I trust your judgment on..."

- **Explanation:** Empowers team members to make decisions within their area of expertise, which builds confidence and ownership.

- **Example:** "**I trust your judgment on** the technical approach. You're the expert here, and I know you'll make the right call."

Expression: "The success of this project depends on..."

- **Explanation:** Clearly communicates what's most critical for success, helping team members prioritize their efforts effectively.

- **Example:** "**The success of this project depends on** clear communication with the client and staying within budget. Everything else is secondary."

3. Providing Direction During Uncertainty

These phrases help you guide your team through challenging or ambiguous situations with confidence.

Expression: "Here's what we know, and here's what we don't know."

- **Explanation:** Provides honest transparency about the situation, which builds trust and helps the team make informed decisions.

- **Example:** "**Here's what we know:** the client wants to launch by Q4. **Here's what we don't know:** their exact budget and technical requirements. Let's focus on what we can control."

Expression: "Our priority right now is..."

- **Explanation:** Provides clear focus during uncertain times, helping the team concentrate their efforts on what matters most.

- **Example:** "There's a lot of uncertainty in the market right now. **Our priority right now is** maintaining excellent customer service and protecting our existing relationships."

Expression: "We'll figure this out together."

- **Explanation:** Creates a sense of unity and shared problem-solving, reducing anxiety and building team cohesion.

- **Example:** "This is a complex challenge, and I don't have all the answers yet. But **we'll figure this out together.** We have a smart, experienced team."

Expression: "Let's focus on what we can control."

- **Explanation:** Redirects energy from worrying about external factors to taking productive action on things within the team's influence.

- **Example:** "The economic situation is uncertain, but **let's focus on what we can control:** delivering excellent work and building strong client relationships."

4. Building Accountability and Ownership

These phrases help create a culture where team members take responsibility for results and continuous improvement.

Expression: "What do you think we should do?"

- **Explanation:** Encourages team members to think strategically and take ownership of solutions rather than just following orders.

- **Example:** "We're behind schedule on the project. **What do you think we should do** to get back on track?"

Expression: "How can we improve this process?"

- **Explanation:** Promotes continuous improvement and shows that you value the team's input on making things better.

- **Example:** "The client feedback was mostly positive, but there were some concerns about our response time. **How can we improve this process** for next time?"

Expression: "What did we learn from this?"

- **Explanation:** Turns mistakes and setbacks into learning opportunities, creating a culture that embraces growth and improvement.

- **Example:** "The product launch didn't go as smoothly as we hoped. **What did we learn from this** that we can apply to future launches?"

Expression: "I need you to own this."

- **Explanation:** Clearly assigns ownership and accountability for specific outcomes, ensuring someone is responsible for results.

- **Example:** "Customer satisfaction scores are declining in the Northeast region. Mike, **I need you to own this** and develop a plan to turn it around."

5. Recognizing and Celebrating Success

These phrases help you acknowledge achievements and reinforce positive behaviors that drive continued success.

Expression: "I'm proud of what we've accomplished."

- **Explanation:** Shows personal investment in the team's success and creates a sense of shared achievement.

- **Example:** "**I'm proud of what we've accomplished** this quarter. We not only met our targets but exceeded them by 15%."

Expression: "This is exactly the kind of thinking we need."

- **Explanation:** Reinforces specific behaviors or approaches you want to see more of from the team.

- **Example:** "Sarah's suggestion to survey customers before finalizing the design is **exactly the kind of thinking we need.** It shows we're putting customers first."

Expression: "You've set a new standard for..."

- **Explanation:** Recognizes exceptional performance while setting expectations for future work.

- **Example:** "The way you handled that difficult client situation, Tom, **you've set a new standard for** customer service excellence."

Scenario: Team Meeting After a Successful Project

Leader: "**I'm proud of what we've accomplished** with the Johnson project. We delivered on time, under budget, and the client is thrilled." **Team Member:** "It was definitely a team effort. Everyone stepped up when we hit those technical challenges." **Leader:** "Absolutely. And Lisa, your decision to bring in the external consultant early was **exactly the kind of thinking we need.** It prevented what could have been a major delay." **Lisa:** "Thanks. I just wanted to make sure we had all the expertise we needed." **Leader: "You've set a new standard for** proactive problem-solving. **What did we learn from this** that we can apply to the next project?"

Common Mistakes and How to Avoid Them

Mistake 1: Micromanaging Through Language. Using phrases like "Make sure you..." or "Don't forget to..." can make team members feel like you don't trust them.

- **How to Avoid:** Use empowering language like "I trust your judgment on..." and "I'm counting on you to..." that shows confidence in their abilities.

Mistake 2: Taking Credit for Team Success. Using "I" instead of "we" when discussing achievements can demoralize your team and damage relationships.

- **How to Avoid:** Always use inclusive language like "We accomplished..." and "Our team achieved..." to share credit and build team pride.

Mistake 3: Avoiding Difficult Conversations. Using vague language to avoid addressing performance issues or conflicts can allow problems to grow worse.

- **How to Avoid:** Be direct but supportive with phrases like "I need you to own this" and "How can we improve this process?" to address issues constructively.

Try This: Your Turn to Practice

Scenario: Your team has been working on a challenging project for three months. They've encountered several unexpected obstacles, morale is low, and some team members are starting to doubt whether the project can succeed. You need to address the team and restore confidence while acknowledging the difficulties.

Your Task:

1. How would you acknowledge the challenges while maintaining a positive outlook?

2. How would you motivate the team to continue pushing forward?

3. How would you delegate responsibility for moving forward while showing your support?

(Practice your responses. For example: "I know this project has been more challenging than we expected. Here's what we know: we've solved the major technical issues and the client is still committed. Here's what we don't know: exactly how long the final phase will take. But I have complete confidence in this team. We're going to make a real difference with this project. Sarah, I'm counting on you to lead the final testing phase, and you have my full support. Let's focus on what we can control and finish strong.")

Chapter 10: Key Takeaways

Inspire with Confidence: Use phrases like "I have complete confidence in this team" and "We're going to make a real difference" to build enthusiasm and belief.

Empower Through Delegation: Delegate with phrases like "I'm counting on you to..." and "I trust your judgment on..." to build ownership and accountability.

Lead Through Uncertainty: Provide clarity with "Here's what we know..." and "Our priority right now is..." to guide teams through challenging times.

Build Ownership: Use questions like "What do you think we should do?" and "How can we improve this?" to encourage strategic thinking and continuous improvement.

Celebrate Success: Recognize achievements with "I'm proud of what we've accomplished" and "You've set a new standard for..." to reinforce positive behaviors.

CHAPTER TEN

Negotiating and Persuading Successfully

Negotiation and persuasion are essential skills in virtually every aspect of business, from closing sales and securing partnerships to managing budgets and resolving conflicts. Whether you're negotiating a contract with a major client, persuading your team to adopt a new process, or trying to secure additional resources for your department, your success often depends on your ability to influence others through strategic communication. The best negotiators and persuaders aren't necessarily the most aggressive or manipulative—they're the ones who understand how to build rapport, find mutual benefits, and guide conversations toward win-win outcomes. This chapter provides you with the essential phrases and expressions that will help you become more effective at influencing others, reaching agreements, and achieving your objectives while maintaining positive relationships.

Essential Expressions for Negotiation and Persuasion

Here are the key phrases for every aspect of negotiation and persuasion, from building rapport to closing deals. Each is explained with a simple definition and a realistic usage example.

1. Building Rapport and Finding Common Ground

These phrases help you establish trust and identify shared interests, which are the foundation of successful negotiations.

Expression: "I think we both want..."

- **Explanation:** Identifies shared goals or interests, creating a collaborative foundation for the negotiation rather than an adversarial one.//
- **Example:** "**I think we both want** to find a solution that works for both companies and creates long-term value."

Expression: "We're on the same side here."

- **Explanation:** Reinforces the idea that you're working together toward a common goal rather than fighting against each other.
- **Example:** "**We're on the same side here.** We both want this project to succeed and deliver results for your customers."

Expression: "I understand your position."

- **Explanation:** Shows empathy and acknowledgment of the other party's perspective, which builds trust and opens them to hearing your viewpoint.
- **Example:** "**I understand your position** on the timeline. You need to launch before the holiday season to maximize sales."

Expression: "That makes perfect sense from your perspective."

- **Explanation:** Validates the other party's reasoning without necessarily agreeing with their conclusion. It shows you're listening and thinking strategically.

- **Example:** "That makes perfect sense from your perspective. As the CFO, you need to ensure we're getting the best possible return on investment."

2. Presenting Your Position Persuasively

These phrases help you make your case in a way that's compelling and difficult to dismiss.

Expression: "Here's what I'm thinking..."

- **Explanation:** A collaborative way to introduce your proposal that invites discussion rather than demanding acceptance.

- **Example:** "Here's what I'm thinking: What if we structured the payment terms to give you more flexibility in the first quarter?"

Expression: "The way I see it..."

- **Explanation:** Presents your perspective as one valid viewpoint among others, making it easier for the other party to consider without feeling pressured.

- **Example:** "**The way I see it**, this partnership could help both companies expand into new markets more quickly than we could alone."

Expression: "What if we could..."

- **Explanation:** Introduces creative solutions or alternatives in a hypothetical way that feels less threatening and more exploratory.

- **Example:** "**What if we could** find a way to reduce the upfront costs while still meeting your quality requirements?"

Expression: "Consider this..."

- **Explanation:** Asks the other party to think about a new idea or perspective without demanding immediate agreement.

- **Example:** "**Consider this:** by investing in the premium package now, you'll save 30% compared to upgrading later."

3. Exploring Options and Creating Value

These phrases help you move beyond initial positions to find creative solutions that benefit everyone.

Expression: "What would it take for you to...?"

- **Explanation:** A powerful question that uncovers the other party's real needs and constraints, opening the door to creative solutions.

- **Example:** "**What would it take for you to** consider extending the contract for another year?"

Expression: "Is there any flexibility on...?"

- **Explanation:** A polite way to test whether certain terms are negotiable without being too direct or aggressive.

- **Example:** "**Is there any flexibility on** the delivery timeline? We could offer a discount for a slightly longer schedule."

Expression: "Let's explore some options."

- **Explanation:** Suggests collaborative problem-solving and moves the conversation from positions to possibilities.

- **Example:** "I can see we have different priorities here. **Let's explore some options** that might work for both of us."

Expression: "What matters most to you in this deal?"

- **Explanation:** Helps you understand the other party's priorities so you can structure an offer that addresses their key concerns.

- **Example:** "**What matters most to you in this deal?** Is it the price, the timeline, or the ongoing support?"

4. Making Concessions and Trade-offs

These phrases help you give and take strategically while maintaining the value of your position.

Expression: "I could be flexible on... if you could..."

- **Explanation:** Structures a conditional concession that requires something in return, maintaining balance in the negotiation.

- **Example:** "**I could be flexible on** the payment terms **if you could** commit to a longer contract period."

Expression: "In exchange for..."

- **Explanation:** Clearly links concessions to reciprocal benefits, ensuring that any give-and-take is balanced and fair.

- **Example:** "**In exchange for** the volume discount you're requesting, we'd need a minimum order commitment."

Expression: "That's something I'd have to think about."

- **Explanation:** Buys you time to consider an offer without rejecting it outright, keeping the negotiation moving forward.

- **Example:** "A 20% discount is significant. **That's something I'd have to think about** and discuss with my team."

Expression: "I can work with that if..."

- **Explanation:** Shows willingness to accept their proposal while introducing your own conditions or modifications.

- **Example:** "**I can work with that timeline if** we can adjust the scope slightly to focus on the most critical features first."

5. Closing and Securing Agreement

These phrases help you move from discussion to commitment and finalize agreements.

Expression: "So, if I understand correctly, we're agreeing to..."

- **Explanation:** Summarizes the key points of agreement to ensure everyone is on the same page before finalizing.

- **Example:** "**So, if I understand correctly, we're agreeing to** a 12-month contract with quarterly reviews and a 10% discount for early payment."

Expression: "Are we in agreement on...?"

- **Explanation:** Seeks explicit confirmation on specific points to avoid misunderstandings later.

- **Example:** "**Are we in agreement on** the delivery schedule and the payment terms we just discussed?"

Expression: "I think we have a deal."

- **Explanation:** A confident statement that signals you believe you've reached a mutually acceptable agreement.

- **Example:** "With those modifications to the contract terms, **I think we have a deal.** Should we move forward with the paperwork?"

Expression: "Let's move forward with this."

- **Explanation:** A decisive phrase that transitions from negotiation to implementation, showing commitment to the agreement.

- **Example:** "This proposal addresses all our key concerns. **Let's move forward with this** and get the contracts drafted."

Scenario: Contract Negotiation

Buyer: "The price is higher than we budgeted for this project." **Seller:** "**I understand your position** on the budget constraints. **What matters most to you in this deal**—is it the total cost or the payment schedule?" **Buyer:** "It's really about cash flow. We need to spread the payments out over a longer period." **Seller:** "Here's what I'm thinking: **What if we could** structure it as quarterly payments over 18 months instead of the standard 12?" **Buyer:** "That could work. **What would it take for you to** keep the same total price with that payment schedule?" **Seller:** "**I could be flexible on** the payment terms **if you could** commit to a two-year service agreement instead of one year." **Buyer:** "**That's something I'd have to think about.** Let me discuss it with my team and get back to you tomorrow." **Seller:** "Of course. Take your time. **I think we both want** to find a solution that works for everyone."

Common Mistakes and How to Avoid Them

Mistake 1: Making the First Offer Too Aggressive. Starting with an extreme position can damage rapport and make the other party defensive or unwilling to negotiate.

- **How to Avoid:** Begin with reasonable offers and use phrases like "Here's what I'm thinking..." to present proposals as starting points for discussion rather than final demands.

Mistake 2: Focusing Only on Your Own Needs. Talking only about what you want without considering the other party's interests makes it difficult to reach mutually beneficial agreements.

- **How to Avoid:** Use phrases like "What matters most to you?" and "I understand your position" to show you're considering their needs and constraints.

Mistake 3: Making Concessions Without Getting Anything in Return. Giving away value without receiving reciprocal benefits weakens your negotiating position and can lead to one-sided agreements.

- **How to Avoid:** Always structure concessions conditionally using phrases like "I could be flexible on... if you could..." to ensure balanced exchanges.

Try This: Your Turn to Practice

Scenario: You're negotiating with a potential client who loves your proposal but says your price is 25% higher than your main competitor's quote. They want to work with you but need you to match the competitor's price. You believe your service is worth the premium, but you don't want to lose the deal.

Your Task:

1. How would you acknowledge their position while defending your value?

2. What questions could you ask to understand their priorities and find room for negotiation?

3. How would you propose a creative solution that doesn't simply match the competitor's price?

(Practice your responses. For example: "I understand your position on the pricing—budget is always a key consideration. What matters most to you in this partnership beyond the initial cost? What if we could structure this differently—perhaps we could match their price for the first phase if you could commit to a longer-term agreement that includes additional services?")

Chapter 11: Key Takeaways

Build Rapport First: Use phrases like "I think we both want..." and "We're on the same side here" to establish collaborative foundations.

Present Ideas Collaboratively: Introduce proposals with "Here's what I'm thinking..." and "What if we could..." to invite discussion rather than demand acceptance.

Explore Creative Solutions: Ask "What would it take for you to..." and "What matters most to you?" to uncover opportunities for mutual benefit.

Make Balanced Exchanges: Structure concessions with "I could be flexible on... if you could..." to ensure fair trade-offs.

Close with Clarity: Use "So, if I understand correctly..." and "Are we in agreement on..." to confirm understanding before finalizing agreements.

CHAPTER ELEVEN

Excelling in International Business

In today's interconnected global economy, the ability to communicate effectively across cultures is not just an advantage—it's essential for success. Whether you're working with international clients, managing remote teams across different time zones, or expanding your business into new markets, your success depends on your ability to navigate cultural differences, avoid misunderstandings, and build trust with people from diverse backgrounds. International business communication requires more than just speaking the same language; it demands cultural sensitivity, clarity, and an understanding of how different cultures approach business relationships, decision-making, and communication styles. This chapter provides you with the essential phrases and expressions that will help you excel in global business environments while respecting cultural differences and building strong international partnerships.

Essential Expressions for International Business

Here are the key phrases for communicating effectively in global business contexts, with special attention to cultural sensitivity and clarity. Each is explained with a simple definition and a realistic usage example.

1. Building Cross-Cultural Rapport

These phrases help you establish positive relationships with international colleagues and clients while showing cultural awareness.

Expression: "I hope I'm not calling at an inconvenient time."

- **Explanation:** Shows awareness of time zone differences and respect for the other person's schedule, which is crucial in international business.

- **Example:** "Good morning, Mr. Tanaka. **I hope I'm not calling at an inconvenient time.** I know it's quite late in Tokyo."

Expression: "Please correct me if I'm mispronouncing your name."

- **Explanation:** Shows respect for the person's identity and cultural background while acknowledging that you want to get it right.

- **Example:** "It's a pleasure to meet you, Ms. Kowalski. **Please correct me if I'm mispronouncing your name**—I want to make sure I say it properly."

Expression: "I understand business practices may be different in your country."

- **Explanation:** Acknowledges cultural differences in business approaches and shows openness to learning about other ways of doing business.

- **Example:** "**I understand business practices may be different in your country.** Could you help me understand the typical decision-making process for projects like this?"

Expression: "I'd love to learn more about how things work in [country/region]."

- **Explanation:** Shows genuine interest in understanding cultural and business differences, which builds rapport and demonstrates respect.

- **Example:** "**I'd love to learn more about how things work in** the German market. What are the key factors customers consider when choosing a supplier?"

2. Ensuring Clear Communication

These phrases help prevent misunderstandings that can arise from language barriers or cultural differences in communication styles.

Expression: "Let me make sure I understand correctly..."

- **Explanation:** A crucial phrase for international communication that helps verify understanding and prevents costly misunderstandings.

- **Example:** "**Let me make sure I understand correctly**—you need the proposal by next Friday, and it should include pricing for both the basic and premium packages?"

Expression: "Could you help me understand what you mean by...?"

- **Explanation:** A polite way to ask for clarification when terms or concepts might have different meanings in different cultures or contexts.

- **Example:** "Could you help me understand what you mean by 'flexible timeline'? Are we talking about days, weeks, or months of flexibility?"

Expression: "To avoid any confusion..."

- **Explanation:** Proactively addresses potential misunderstandings by being extra clear about important details.

- **Example:** "To avoid any confusion, when I say 'next week,' I mean the week of March 15th, not this coming week."

Expression: "I want to be very clear about..."

- **Explanation:** Emphasizes important points that must be understood correctly, especially when dealing with contracts or commitments.

- **Example:** "I want to be very clear about the delivery terms. The goods will be delivered to your warehouse in Shanghai, not to the port."

3. Showing Cultural Sensitivity

These phrases demonstrate respect for cultural differences and help you navigate potentially sensitive topics.

Expression: "I hope this aligns with your expectations."

- **Explanation:** Shows consideration for different cultural expectations and business practices without making assumptions.

- **Example:** "I've prepared a detailed project timeline with weekly check-ins. **I hope this aligns with your expectations** for project management."

Expression: "Please let me know if there's a better way to approach this."

- **Explanation:** Shows humility and openness to different ways of doing business, which is appreciated in many cultures.

- **Example:** "I've outlined our standard contract terms. **Please let me know if there's a better way to approach this** that works with your company's procedures."

Expression: "I respect that you may need time to consider this."

- **Explanation:** Acknowledges that decision-making processes vary across cultures, with some requiring more consultation or deliberation.

- **Example:** "This is a significant investment decision. **I respect that you may need time to consider this** and discuss it with your team."

Expression: "What would be the most appropriate way to...?"

- **Explanation:** Asks for guidance on cultural or business protocols, showing respect for local customs and practices.

- **Example: "What would be the most appropriate way to** follow up on this proposal? Should I contact you directly or work through your assistant?"

4. Managing Time Zone and Scheduling Challenges

These phrases help you coordinate effectively across different time zones and work schedules.

Expression: "What time works best for you in your time zone?"

- **Explanation:** Shows consideration for the other person's local time and work schedule rather than assuming they'll accommodate yours.

- **Example:** "I'd like to schedule a call to discuss the project details. **What time works best for you in your time zone?** I'm flexible with my schedule."

Expression: "I know it's early/late for you."

- **Explanation:** Acknowledges the inconvenience of time zone differences and shows appreciation for their flexibility.

- **Example:** "Thank you for joining the call this morning. **I know it's quite early for you** in Sydney, and I appreciate your flexibility."

Expression: "Should we find a time that's more convenient for everyone?"

- **Explanation:** Suggests finding meeting times that work better for all parties, especially in multi-time-zone situations.

- **Example:** "I realize this 6 AM call is challenging for our Tokyo team. **Should we find a time that's more convenient for everyone?**"

Expression: "I'll send a calendar invitation with the time in all relevant time zones."

- **Explanation:** Proactively prevents confusion by clearly stating meeting times in multiple time zones.

- **Example:** "**I'll send a calendar invitation with the time in all relevant time zones** so everyone knows exactly when to join."

5. Navigating Business Etiquette Differences

These phrases help you handle situations where business customs and expectations may differ across cultures.

Expression: "I want to make sure I'm following proper protocol."

- **Explanation:** Shows respect for local business customs and your desire to conduct business appropriately.

- **Example:** "Before we begin the presentation, **I want to make sure I'm following proper protocol.** Should I address questions during the presentation or wait until the end?"

Expression: "Please feel free to interrupt if you have questions."

- **Explanation:** Encourages participation from cultures where interrupting might be considered rude, ensuring everyone feels comfortable engaging.

- **Example:** "I'll be presenting for about 20 minutes. **Please feel free to interrupt if you have questions**—I want this to be interactive."

Expression: "I understand this may require approval from senior management."

- **Explanation:** Acknowledges hierarchical decision-making structures that are common in many cultures.

- **Example:** "This is a significant contract change. **I understand this may require approval from senior management.** What's the typical process for getting that approval?"

Scenario: International Client Meeting

US Manager: "Good morning everyone. **I hope I'm not calling at an inconvenient time** for our colleagues in Asia." **Japanese Client:** "Good evening from Tokyo. Thank you for accommodating our schedule." **US Manager:** "Of course. **I know it's quite late for you**, and we appreciate your flexibility. Before we start, **I want to make sure I'm following proper protocol.** Would you prefer a formal presentation or a more interactive discussion?" **Japanese Client:** "A formal presentation would be appropriate, with questions at the end." **US Manager:** "Perfect. **Let me make sure I understand correctly**—you're looking for a solution that can be implemented across all your Asian offices, correct?" **Japanese Client:** "Yes, that's right. **I understand this may require approval from senior management** on your side as well." **US Manager:** "**I respect that you may need time to consider this** after the presentation. **What would be the most appropriate way to** follow up with additional information?"

Common Mistakes and How to Avoid Them

Mistake 1: Using Idioms and Slang. Expressions like "ballpark figure," "touch base," or "circle back" can confuse non-native speakers and create misunderstandings.

- **How to Avoid:** Use clear, direct language instead. Say "approximate cost" instead of "ballpark figure" and "contact you" instead of "touch base."

Mistake 2: Speaking Too Fast or Using Complex Sentences. Rapid speech and complicated sentence structures can be difficult for non-native speakers to follow.

- **How to Avoid:** Speak slowly and clearly, use shorter sentences, and pause frequently to allow for processing time. Check for understanding regularly.

Mistake 3: Making Cultural Assumptions. Assuming that business practices, communication styles, or decision-making processes are the same everywhere can lead to misunderstandings and offense.

- **How to Avoid:** Ask questions about local practices and preferences using phrases like "I understand business practices may be different in your country" and "What would be the most appropriate way to...?"

Try This: Your Turn to Practice

Scenario: You're leading a video conference with team members from the US, Germany, Japan, and Brazil to discuss a new product launch. The German team prefers detailed planning, the Japanese team needs time for consensus-building, the Brazilian team values relationship-building, and you need to coordinate across multiple time zones.

Your Task:

1. How would you open the meeting to acknowledge the international nature of the team?
2. How would you ensure everyone understands the key decisions that need to be made?
3. How would you respect different cultural approaches to decision-making while keeping the project moving forward?

(Practice your responses. For example: "Good morning, good afternoon, and good evening everyone, depending on your time zone. I know it's quite early for our colleagues in Brazil and late for our team in Japan, so I appreciate everyone's flexibility. Let me make sure I understand correctly what we need to accomplish today... I understand this may require different approval processes in each region, so please let me know what would be the most appropriate way to move forward in your markets.")

Chapter 12: Key Takeaways

Show Cultural Awareness: Use phrases like "I hope I'm not calling at an inconvenient time" and "I understand business practices may be different in your country" to demonstrate respect for cultural differences.

Ensure Clear Communication: Regularly check understanding with "Let me make sure I understand correctly..." and "Could you help me understand what you mean by...?" to prevent misunderstandings.

Respect Different Approaches: Acknowledge varying business practices with "I respect that you may need time to consider this" and "What would be the most appropriate way to...?"

Coordinate Across Time Zones: Show consideration with "What time works best for you in your time zone?" and "I know it's early/late for you" when scheduling international meetings.

Avoid Cultural Assumptions: Ask about local practices and preferences rather than assuming your way of doing business is universal.

CHAPTER TWELVE

Communicating Effectively in a Virtual World

The digital transformation of the workplace has fundamentally changed how we communicate professionally. Virtual meetings, remote collaboration, and digital communication platforms have become the norm rather than the exception. While technology has made it easier to connect with colleagues and clients around the world, it has also created new challenges for effective communication. Without the benefit of full body language, casual hallway conversations, and in-person relationship building, professionals must adapt their communication style to succeed in virtual environments. This chapter provides you with the essential phrases and expressions that will help you excel in digital communication. You will learn how to run effective virtual meetings, collaborate seamlessly with remote teams, maintain professional relationships online, and handle the unique challenges that come with communicating through screens and digital platforms.

Essential Expressions for Virtual Communication

Here are the key phrases for every aspect of virtual communication, from video calls to digital collaboration. Each is explained with a simple definition and a realistic usage example.

1. Managing Virtual Meetings Effectively

These phrases help you run smooth, productive virtual meetings and ensure everyone can participate effectively.

Expression: "Can everyone see my screen clearly?"

- **Explanation:** A crucial check when sharing presentations or documents to ensure all participants can follow along with visual content.

- **Example:** "I'm going to share the quarterly report now. **Can everyone see my screen clearly?** Let me know if you need me to make anything larger."

Expression: "I'm going to mute myself while you're speaking."

- **Explanation:** Shows consideration for audio quality and prevents background noise from disrupting the speaker.

- **Example:** "**I'm going to mute myself while you're speaking** to avoid any background noise from my end."

Expression: "Could you repeat that? I think we lost you for a moment."

- **Explanation:** A polite way to address technical issues like poor audio or video connection without making the speaker feel bad.

- **Example:** "Could you repeat that? **I think we lost you for a moment** when you were explaining the timeline."

Expression: "Let's go around the room and hear from everyone."

- **Explanation:** Ensures all participants have a chance to contribute, which is especially important in virtual settings where it's easier for people to stay silent.

- **Example:** "Before we wrap up, **let's go around the room and hear from everyone** about their thoughts on this proposal."

2. Handling Technical Difficulties Gracefully

These phrases help you manage the inevitable technical issues that arise in virtual communication.

Expression: "I'm having some technical difficulties. Bear with me for a moment."

- **Explanation:** Acknowledges technical problems while asking for patience, maintaining professionalism during disruptions.

- **Example:** "**I'm having some technical difficulties. Bear with me for a moment** while I try to reconnect to the call."

Expression: "Can you hear me okay now?"

- **Explanation:** Checks audio quality after experiencing connection issues or making technical adjustments.

- **Example:** "I switched to a different microphone. **Can you hear me okay now?** The audio should be clearer."

Expression: "Should we try calling in by phone instead?"

- **Explanation:** Suggests an alternative when video or internet connection issues are persistent.

- **Example:** "The video keeps freezing on my end. **Should we try calling in by phone instead** to ensure we can continue the discussion?"

Expression: "I'll follow up with the details in an email."

- **Explanation:** Ensures important information isn't lost due to technical issues during the call.

- **Example:** "I know the connection was spotty during that explanation. **I'll follow up with the details in an email** so everyone has the complete information."

3. Facilitating Remote Collaboration

These phrases help coordinate work and maintain productivity when team members are working from different locations.

Expression: "I'll share this document with editing access."

- **Explanation:** Clearly communicates how team members can collaborate on shared documents and what level of access they'll have.

- **Example:** "**I'll share this document with editing access** so everyone can add their comments and suggestions directly."

Expression: "Let's set up a shared workspace for this project."

- **Explanation:** Suggests creating a centralized location for project files and communication to keep remote teams organized.

- **Example:** "**Let's set up a shared workspace for this project** where we can store all the files and track our progress."

Expression: "I'll update the status in our project management tool."

- **Explanation:** Keeps remote team members informed about progress through digital tracking systems.

- **Example:** "I've completed the market research phase. **I'll update the status in our project management tool** so everyone can see we're ready for the next step."

Expression: "Can we schedule regular check-ins to stay aligned?"

- **Explanation:** Suggests structured communication to maintain coordination and prevent remote team members from feeling disconnected.

- **Example:** "With everyone working remotely, **can we schedule regular check-ins to stay aligned** on priorities and progress?"

4. Maintaining Professional Relationships Virtually

These phrases help you build and maintain relationships when you can't meet in person.

Expression: "How are things going on your end?"

- **Explanation:** A way to check in personally with remote colleagues and show interest in their well-being and work situation.

- **Example:** "Before we dive into the agenda, **how are things going on your end?** I know you've been dealing with some challenging projects lately."

Expression: "I miss our in-person brainstorming sessions."

- **Explanation:** Acknowledges the challenges of remote work while maintaining a positive tone about past collaboration.

- **Example:** "**I miss our in-person brainstorming sessions**, but I think we can still be creative together virtually. Let's try using the whiteboard feature."

Expression: "Let's schedule some time to catch up properly."

- **Explanation:** Suggests dedicated time for relationship building beyond just work-focused meetings.

- **Example:** "We've been so focused on project deadlines lately. **Let's schedule some time to catch up properly** and talk about how things are going overall."

Expression: "I appreciate you being flexible with the virtual format."

- **Explanation:** Acknowledges that virtual communication requires adaptation and shows gratitude for others' efforts to make it work.

- **Example:** "**I appreciate you being flexible with the virtual format.** I know it's not the same as meeting in person, but you've made this collaboration work really well."

5. Professional Digital Communication Etiquette

These phrases help you maintain professionalism in chat, email, and other digital communication platforms.

Expression: "I'll send you a quick message in chat."

- **Explanation:** Indicates you'll use instant messaging for brief, non-urgent communication rather than interrupting with a call.

- **Example:** "I don't want to interrupt your focus time. **I'll send you a quick message in chat** with the information you requested."

Expression: "Is now a good time for a quick call?"

- **Explanation:** Respects others' schedules and current activities before initiating unscheduled virtual conversations.

- **Example:** "I have a question about the client proposal. **Is now a good time for a quick call**, or should we schedule something later?"

Expression: "I'll be away from my computer for the next hour."

- **Explanation:** Communicates availability status to remote colleagues so they know when you're not immediately reachable.

- **Example:** "**I'll be away from my computer for the next hour** for a client meeting. I'll respond to messages when I'm back."

Expression: "Let me know if you'd prefer to discuss this over video call."

- **Explanation:** Offers to escalate from text-based communication to face-to-face virtual interaction for complex topics.

- **Example:** "This email is getting quite long with all the details. **Let me know if you'd prefer to discuss this over video call** instead."

Scenario: Virtual Team Meeting with Technical Issues

Meeting Host: "Good morning everyone. **Can everyone see my screen clearly?** I'm sharing the project timeline." **Team Member 1:** "I can see it perfectly." **Team Member 2:** "**I'm having some technical difficulties. Bear with me for a moment** while I refresh my browser." **Meeting Host:** "No problem. **Could you repeat that? I think we lost you for a moment**, Sarah." **Sarah:** "I was saying that the design phase is complete. **Can you hear me okay now?**" **Meeting Host:** "Yes, much better. **I'll follow up with the details in an email** so everyone has the timeline in writing. Before we continue, **let's go around the room and hear from everyone** about their current project status." **Team Member 3:** "**Should we try calling in by phone instead?** My video keeps freezing." **Meeting Host:** "That's fine. **I appreciate you being flexible with the virtual format.** Let's continue with whoever can stay on video."

Common Mistakes and How to Avoid Them

Mistake 1: Forgetting to Mute When Not Speaking. Background noise from unmuted participants can be very disruptive in virtual meetings.

- **How to Avoid:** Always mute yourself when not speaking and use phrases like "I'm going to mute myself while you're speaking" to show consideration for others.

Mistake 2: Multitasking During Virtual Meetings. Checking email or doing other work during video calls is often visible and shows disrespect for the meeting.

- **How to Avoid:** Give virtual meetings your full attention just as you would in-person meetings. If you must step away, use phrases like "I'll be away from my computer for the next hour."

Mistake 3: Not Checking for Understanding. It's harder to read body language and engagement in virtual settings, making it easier for misunderstandings to go unnoticed.

- **How to Avoid:** Regularly check for understanding with phrases like "Can everyone see my screen clearly?" and "Let's go around the room and hear from everyone."

Try This: Your Turn to Practice

Scenario: You're leading a virtual brainstorming session with your team to develop ideas for a new marketing campaign. Two team members are having audio issues, one person's video keeps freezing, and you need to ensure everyone can contribute effectively despite the technical challenges.

Your Task:

1. How would you address the technical issues while keeping the meeting productive?

2. How would you ensure everyone can participate in the brainstorming despite the technical difficulties?

3. How would you follow up after the meeting to capture all the ideas discussed?

(Practice your responses. For example: "I can see we're having some technical difficulties today. Should we try calling in by phone instead for those having audio issues? Let's use the chat feature as a backup for sharing ideas. I'll follow

up with the details in an email and share a document with editing access so everyone can add any additional thoughts after the meeting.")

Chapter 13: Key Takeaways

Manage Technical Issues Gracefully: Use phrases like "I'm having some technical difficulties. Bear with me for a moment" and "Can you hear me okay now?" to handle inevitable technology problems professionally.

Ensure Inclusive Participation: Regularly check with "Can everyone see my screen clearly?" and "Let's go around the room and hear from everyone" to make sure all participants can engage effectively.

Maintain Professional Relationships: Show personal interest with "How are things going on your end?" and acknowledge challenges with "I appreciate you being flexible with the virtual format."

Coordinate Remote Work Effectively: Use phrases like "I'll share this document with editing access" and "Can we schedule regular check-ins to stay aligned?" to maintain productivity across distances.

Practice Digital Etiquette: Respect others' time and attention with "Is now a good time for a quick call?" and "I'll be away from my computer for the next hour" to communicate availability clearly.

CHAPTER THIRTEEN

Quick-Reference Glossary

Your instant guide to the right expression for any business situation:

How to Use This Glossary

This thematic glossary organizes all the essential expressions from the book by business function and situation. When you need the right phrase for a specific scenario, simply find the relevant category below and choose the expression that best fits your needs. Each expression includes the chapter reference where you can find more detailed explanations and examples.

BUILDING RELATIONSHIPS & RAPPORT

First Meetings & Introductions

- "It's a pleasure to meet you." *(Chapter 1)*
- "I've heard great things about your work." *(Chapter 1)*
- "Thanks for making the time to meet with me." *(Chapter 1)*

- "Excuse me, I don't think we've met." *(Chapter 8)*
- "I've been looking forward to this conversation." *(Chapter 7)*

Small Talk & Conversation Starters

- "How has your week been so far?" *(Chapter 1)*
- "So, what do you do at [Company Name]?" *(Chapter 1)*
- "Are you enjoying the event?" *(Chapter 8)*
- "What brings you to [event/conference]?" *(Chapter 8)*

Networking & Professional Connections

- "I help [target audience] [achieve specific result]." *(Chapter 8)*
- "That's fascinating. Tell me more about..." *(Chapter 8)*
- "I'd love to learn more about your experience with..." *(Chapter 8)*
- "I might be able to help with that." *(Chapter 8)*

EMAIL & WRITTEN COMMUNICATION

Professional Email Openings

- "I hope this email finds you well." *(Chapter 3)*
- "As we discussed..." / "Following up on our conversation..." *(Chapter 3)*

- "I'm writing to..." [inquire about/request/inform you that] *(Chapter 3)*

Making Requests

- "Could you please...?" *(Chapter 3)*

- "I was wondering if you could..." *(Chapter 1)*

- "Would you be able to...?" *(Chapter 1)*

Email Follow-ups

- "Just a gentle reminder that..." *(Chapter 3)*

- "I was wondering if you've had a chance to..." *(Chapter 3)*

- "It was great meeting you at [event]." *(Chapter 8)*

Email Attachments & References

- "Please find attached..." / "I've attached..." *(Chapter 3)*

- "I thought you might find this interesting..." *(Chapter 8)*

MEETINGS & DISCUSSIONS

Meeting Participation

- "I completely agree with [Name]." *(Chapter 4)*

- "Building on what [Name] said..." *(Chapter 4)*

- "That's exactly my thinking." *(Chapter 4)*

Diplomatic Disagreement

- "I see your point, but..." *(Chapter 4)*
- "I have a slightly different perspective on this." *(Chapter 4)*
- "Have we considered...?" *(Chapter 4)*

Asking for Clarification

- "Could you elaborate on that?" *(Chapter 4)*
- "I want to make sure I understand..." *(Chapter 4)*
- "Can you walk us through...?" *(Chapter 4)*

Contributing Ideas

- "I'd like to suggest..." *(Chapter 4)*
- "What if we...?" *(Chapter 4)*
- "From my experience..." *(Chapter 4)*

PROJECT MANAGEMENT

Delegating Tasks

- "Could you take the lead on...?" *(Chapter 5)*

- "I'd like you to handle..." *(Chapter 5)*
- "This would be right up your alley." *(Chapter 5)*

Progress Reporting

- "We're on track to..." *(Chapter 5)*
- "We've hit a snag with..." *(Chapter 5)*
- "We're ahead of schedule" / "We're behind schedule" *(Chapter 5)*
- "The bottleneck is..." *(Chapter 5)*

Timeline Management

- "The deadline is tight, but doable." *(Chapter 5)*
- "We're cutting it close." *(Chapter 5)*
- "We need to push back the deadline." *(Chapter 5)*
- "If we stick to the timeline..." *(Chapter 5)*

Problem-Solving

- "Let's put our heads together." *(Chapter 5)*
- "What's our best option here?" *(Chapter 5)*
- "Let's brainstorm some alternatives." *(Chapter 5)*
- "We need a workaround." *(Chapter 5)*

DIFFICULT CONVERSATIONS & FEEDBACK

Giving Constructive Feedback

- "I've noticed that..." / "I've observed that..." *(Chapter 6)*
- "I'd like to see..." / "It would be great if..." *(Chapter 6)*
- "Moving forward..." *(Chapter 6)*

Receiving Feedback

- "I appreciate the feedback." *(Chapter 6)*
- "You're absolutely right." *(Chapter 6)*
- "How can I improve this?" *(Chapter 6)*

Declining Requests

- "I'm afraid I don't have the bandwidth right now." *(Chapter 6)*
- "I wish I could help, but..." *(Chapter 6)*
- "That's outside my area of expertise." *(Chapter 6)*
- "No worries if not." *(Chapter 1)*

De-escalating Conflict

- "I can see your point of view." *(Chapter 6)*

- "Let's take a step back." *(Chapter 6)*

- "I understand your frustration." *(Chapter 6)*

- "Let's find a solution that works for everyone." *(Chapter 6)*

JOB INTERVIEWS

Interview Openings

- "Thank you for taking the time to meet with me today." *(Chapter 7)*

- "I'm thrilled to be here." *(Chapter 7)*

- "I've been looking forward to this conversation." *(Chapter 7)*

Answering Questions

- "In my previous role..." / "In my experience..." *(Chapter 7)*

- "What I found particularly rewarding was..." *(Chapter 7)*

- "I'm particularly proud of..." *(Chapter 7)*

- "That's a great question. Let me think about that for a moment." *(Chapter 7)*

Asking Interview Questions

- "I'm curious about..." *(Chapter 7)*

- "What does success look like in this role?" *(Chapter 7)*

- "What are the biggest challenges facing the team right now?" *(Chapter 7)*

- "How would you describe the company culture?" *(Chapter 7)*

Showing Interest

- "That aligns perfectly with my experience in..." *(Chapter 7)*

- "I'd love the opportunity to..." *(Chapter 7)*

- "Based on what you've told me..." *(Chapter 7)*

PRESENTATIONS & PUBLIC SPEAKING

Engaging Openings

- "Thank you all for being here today." *(Chapter 9)*

- "I'm excited to share with you..." *(Chapter 9)*

- "By the end of this presentation, you'll..." *(Chapter 9)*

- "Let me start with a question..." *(Chapter 9)*

Clear Transitions

- "Now that we've covered..., let's move on to..." *(Chapter 9)*

- "This brings me to my next point..." *(Chapter 9)*

- "To put this in perspective..." *(Chapter 9)*
- "The key takeaway here is..." *(Chapter 9)*

Maintaining Engagement

- "As you can see on this slide..." *(Chapter 9)*
- "This is particularly important because..." *(Chapter 9)*
- "Let me give you a concrete example..." *(Chapter 9)*
- "I want to emphasize that..." *(Chapter 9)*

Handling Questions

- "That's an excellent question." *(Chapter 9)*
- "I'm glad you brought that up." *(Chapter 9)*
- "Let me address that in two parts..." *(Chapter 9)*
- "I'll come back to that at the end." *(Chapter 9)*

Strong Closings

- "To summarize the key points..." *(Chapter 9)*
- "The next steps are..." *(Chapter 9)*
- "I encourage you to..." *(Chapter 9)*
- "Thank you for your attention. I'm happy to take any questions."

(Chapter 9)

LEADERSHIP & MOTIVATION

Motivating Teams

- "I have complete confidence in this team." *(Chapter 10)*

- "We're going to make a real difference here." *(Chapter 10)*

- "This is our opportunity to..." *(Chapter 10)*

- "I believe in what we're doing here." *(Chapter 10)*

Empowering Delegation

- "I'm counting on you to..." *(Chapter 10)*

- "You have my full support on this." *(Chapter 10)*

- "I trust your judgment on..." *(Chapter 10)*

- "The success of this project depends on..." *(Chapter 10)*

Leading Through Uncertainty

- "Here's what we know, and here's what we don't know." *(Chapter 10)*

- "Our priority right now is..." *(Chapter 10)*

- "We'll figure this out together." *(Chapter 10)*

- "Let's focus on what we can control." *(Chapter 10)*

Building Accountability

- "What do you think we should do?" *(Chapter 10)*
- "How can we improve this process?" *(Chapter 10)*
- "What did we learn from this?" *(Chapter 10)*
- "I need you to own this." *(Chapter 10)*

Recognizing Success

- "I'm proud of what we've accomplished." *(Chapter 10)*
- "This is exactly the kind of thinking we need." *(Chapter 10)*
- "You've set a new standard for..." *(Chapter 10)*

NEGOTIATION & PERSUASION

Building Common Ground

- "I think we both want..." *(Chapter 11)*
- "We're on the same side here." *(Chapter 11)*
- "I understand your position." *(Chapter 11)*
- "That makes perfect sense from your perspective." *(Chapter 11)*

Presenting Your Position

- "Here's what I'm thinking..." *(Chapter 11)*
- "The way I see it..." *(Chapter 11)*
- "What if we could..." *(Chapter 11)*
- "Consider this..." *(Chapter 11)*

Exploring Options

- "What would it take for you to...?" *(Chapter 11)*
- "Is there any flexibility on...?" *(Chapter 11)*
- "Let's explore some options." *(Chapter 11)*
- "What matters most to you in this deal?" *(Chapter 11)*

Making Trade-offs

- "I could be flexible on... if you could..." *(Chapter 11)*
- "In exchange for..." *(Chapter 11)*
- "That's something I'd have to think about." *(Chapter 11)*
- "I can work with that if..." *(Chapter 11)*

Closing Deals

- "So, if I understand correctly, we're agreeing to..." *(Chapter 11)*

- "Are we in agreement on...?" *(Chapter 11)*

- "I think we have a deal." *(Chapter 11)*

- "Let's move forward with this." *(Chapter 11)*

INTERNATIONAL BUSINESS

Cross-Cultural Rapport

- "I hope I'm not calling at an inconvenient time." *(Chapter 12)*

- "Please correct me if I'm mispronouncing your name." *(Chapter 12)*

- "I understand business practices may be different in your country." *(Chapter 12)*

- "I'd love to learn more about how things work in [country/region]." *(Chapter 12)*

Ensuring Clear Communication

- "Let me make sure I understand correctly..." *(Chapter 12)*

- "Could you help me understand what you mean by...?" *(Chapter 12)*

- "To avoid any confusion..." *(Chapter 12)*

- "I want to be very clear about..." *(Chapter 12)*

Cultural Sensitivity

- "I hope this aligns with your expectations." *(Chapter 12)*

- "Please let me know if there's a better way to approach this." *(Chapter 12)*

- "I respect that you may need time to consider this." *(Chapter 12)*

- "What would be the most appropriate way to...?" *(Chapter 12)*

Time Zone Coordination

- "What time works best for you in your time zone?" *(Chapter 12)*

- "I know it's early/late for you." *(Chapter 12)*

- "Should we find a time that's more convenient for everyone?" *(Chapter 12)*

- "I'll send a calendar invitation with the time in all relevant time zones." *(Chapter 12)*

VIRTUAL COMMUNICATION

Virtual Meeting Management

- "Can everyone see my screen clearly?" *(Chapter 13)*

- "I'm going to mute myself while you're speaking." *(Chapter 13)*

- "Could you repeat that? I think we lost you for a moment."

(Chapter 13)

- "Let's go around the room and hear from everyone." *(Chapter 13)*

Technical Difficulties

- "I'm having some technical difficulties. Bear with me for a moment." *(Chapter 13)*

- "Can you hear me okay now?" *(Chapter 13)*

- "Should we try calling in by phone instead?" *(Chapter 13)*

- "I'll follow up with the details in an email." *(Chapter 13)*

Remote Collaboration

- "I'll share this document with editing access." *(Chapter 13)*

- "Let's set up a shared workspace for this project." *(Chapter 13)*

- "I'll update the status in our project management tool." *(Chapter 13)*

- "Can we schedule regular check-ins to stay aligned?" *(Chapter 13)*

Virtual Relationship Building

- "How are things going on your end?" *(Chapter 13)*

- "I miss our in-person brainstorming sessions." *(Chapter 13)*

- "Let's schedule some time to catch up properly." *(Chapter 13)*
- "I appreciate you being flexible with the virtual format." *(Chapter 13)*

Digital Etiquette

- "I'll send you a quick message in chat." *(Chapter 13)*
- "Is now a good time for a quick call?" *(Chapter 13)*
- "I'll be away from my computer for the next hour." *(Chapter 13)*
- "Let me know if you'd prefer to discuss this over video call." *(Chapter 13)*

CLARITY & CONFIRMATION

Stating Your Message Clearly

- "In short..." / "To put it simply..." *(Chapter 2)*
- "The bottom line is..." *(Chapter 2)*
- "To be clear..." *(Chapter 2)*

Confirming Understanding

- "So, if I understand correctly..." *(Chapter 2)*
- "Let me just repeat that back to you to make sure I have it right." *(Chapter 2)*

- "Are we on the same page?" *(Chapter 2)*

Projecting Confidence

- "That's a great question." *(Chapter 2)*
- "My thinking on this is..." *(Chapter 2)*
- "I'm confident that..." *(Chapter 2)*

FOLLOW-UP & RELATIONSHIP MAINTENANCE

Professional Follow-up

- "It was great meeting you at [event]." *(Chapter 8)*
- "I thought you might find this interesting..." *(Chapter 8)*
- "I'd love to continue our conversation over coffee." *(Chapter 8)*
- "Please don't hesitate to reach out if..." *(Chapter 8)*

Maintaining Connections

- "How are things going on your end?" *(Chapter 13)*
- "Let's schedule some time to catch up properly." *(Chapter 13)*

CHAPTER FOURTEEN

A-Z Glossary

An alphabetical reference of all essential business expressions

How to Use This Glossary

This comprehensive glossary contains every key expression from "Mastering Business English" arranged alphabetically for quick reference. Each entry includes a concise definition, usage example, and chapter reference for more detailed information.

A

"Are we in agreement on...?" (Chapter 11)

Definition: Seeks explicit confirmation on specific negotiation points

Example: "Are we in agreement on the delivery schedule and payment terms?"

"Are we on the same page?" (Chapter 2)

Definition: Asks if everyone understands or agrees on the situation

Example: "So the plan is to launch next month. Are we on the same page?"

"Are you enjoying the event?" (Chapter 8)

Definition: Safe conversation starter for networking situations

Example: "Hi there! Are you enjoying the conference so far?"

"As we discussed..." (Chapter 3)

Definition: References a previous conversation to provide context

Example: "As we discussed in yesterday's meeting, here are the revised numbers."

"As you can see on this slide..." (Chapter 9)

Definition: Directs audience attention to visual presentation elements

Example: "As you can see on this slide, our sales increased by 25%."

B

"Based on what you've told me..." (Chapter 7)

Definition: Shows active listening and ability to synthesize information

Example: "Based on what you've told me about the company's goals, this role seems perfect."

"Building on what [Name] said..." (Chapter 4)

Definition: Shows agreement while adding additional perspective

Example: "Building on what Sarah said about budget concerns, we should also consider timing."

"By the end of this presentation, you'll..." (Chapter 9)

Definition: Sets clear expectations for presentation outcomes

Example: "By the end of this presentation, you'll understand our new strategy."

C

"Can everyone see my screen clearly?" (Chapter 13)

Definition: Checks visual accessibility in virtual presentations

Example: "I'm sharing the report now. Can everyone see my screen clearly?"

"Can we schedule regular check-ins to stay aligned?" (Chapter 13)

Definition: Suggests structured communication for remote teams

Example: "With everyone working remotely, can we schedule regular check-ins?"

"Can you hear me okay now?" (Chapter 13)

Definition: Checks audio quality after technical adjustments

Example: "I switched microphones. Can you hear me okay now?"

"Can you walk us through...?" (Chapter 4)

Definition: Asks for step-by-step explanation of complex topics

Example: "This sounds promising. Can you walk us through the implementation?"

"Consider this..." (Chapter 11)

Definition: Introduces new ideas without demanding immediate agreement

Example: "Consider this: investing now could save 30% compared to upgrading later."

"Could you elaborate on that?" (Chapter 4)

Definition: Requests more detailed information about a point

Example: "That's interesting. Could you elaborate on how this would work?"

"Could you help me understand what you mean by...?" (Chapter 12)

Definition: Politely asks for clarification on unclear terms

Example: "Could you help me understand what you mean by 'flexible timeline'?"

"Could you please...?" (Chapter 3)

Definition: Polite way to make requests in professional settings

Example: "Could you please send me the updated report when convenient?"

"Could you repeat that? I think we lost you for a moment." (Chapter 13)

Definition: Addresses technical issues without blaming the speaker

Example: "Could you repeat that? I think we lost you during the connection issue."

"Could you take the lead on...?" (Chapter 5)

Definition: Assigns primary responsibility while showing trust

Example: "Sarah, could you take the lead on the customer research phase?"

E

"Excuse me, I don't think we've met." (Chapter 8)

Definition: Professional way to introduce yourself to strangers

Example: "Excuse me, I don't think we've met. I'm David from Marketing."

F

"Following up on our conversation..." (Chapter 3)

Definition: References previous discussion to provide email context

Example: "Following up on our conversation, I've attached the proposal."

"From my experience..." (Chapter 4)

Definition: Shares insights based on personal background

Example: "From my experience with similar projects, this approach works well."

H

"Have we considered...?" (Chapter 4)

Definition: Indirect way to challenge ideas or suggest alternatives

Example: "This plan looks good. Have we considered the budget implications?"

"Here's what I'm thinking…" (Chapter 11)

Definition: Collaborative way to introduce proposals for discussion

Example: "Here's what I'm thinking: what if we structured payments quarterly?"

"Here's what we know, and here's what we don't know." (Chapter 10)

Definition: Provides transparent assessment during uncertainty

Example: "Here's what we know: the deadline is firm. Here's what we don't know: the exact requirements."

"How are things going on your end?" (Chapter 13)

Definition: Personal check-in with remote colleagues

Example: "Before we start, how are things going on your end?"

"How can I improve this?" (Chapter 6)

Definition: Proactive response to feedback showing commitment to growth

Example: "I see the presentation was unclear. How can I improve this next time?"

"How has your week been so far?" (Chapter 1)

Definition: Open-ended question for professional small talk

Example: "Good morning, Tom. How has your week been so far?"

"How would you describe the company culture?" (Chapter 7)

Definition: Interview question to assess cultural fit

Example: "How would you describe the company culture here?"

I

"I appreciate the feedback." (Chapter 6)

Definition: Professional acknowledgment of criticism or suggestions

Example: "I appreciate the feedback about my presentation style."

"I appreciate you being flexible with the virtual format." (Chapter 13)

Definition: Acknowledges adaptation required for virtual communication

Example: "I appreciate you being flexible with the virtual format for today's meeting."

"I believe in what we're doing here." (Chapter 10)

Definition: Shows personal conviction to inspire team commitment

Example: "I believe in what we're doing here. This project will transform our industry."

"I can see your point of view." (Chapter 6)

Definition: Acknowledges someone's perspective to reduce defensiveness

Example: "I can see your point of view about the timeline being aggressive."

"I can work with that if..." (Chapter 11)

Definition: Shows willingness to accept proposals with conditions

Example: "I can work with that timeline if we can adjust the scope slightly."

"I completely agree with [Name]." (Chapter 4)

Definition: Shows strong support for someone's point in meetings

Example: "I completely agree with Sarah about focusing on customer experience."

"I could be flexible on... if you could..." (Chapter 11)

Definition: Structures conditional concessions in negotiations

Example: "I could be flexible on payment terms if you could commit to a longer contract."

"I couldn't help but overhear..." (Chapter 8)

Definition: Natural way to join ongoing conversations at events

Example: "I couldn't help but overhear you discussing remote team challenges."

"I encourage you to..." (Chapter 9)

Definition: Motivational closing that suggests specific audience actions

Example: "I encourage you to think about how these strategies apply to your projects."

"I have complete confidence in this team." (Chapter 10)

Definition: Builds team confidence and shows trust in abilities

Example: "This is challenging, but I have complete confidence in this team."

"I help [target audience] [achieve specific result]." (Chapter 8)

Definition: Benefit-focused self-introduction for networking

Example: "I help small businesses streamline their accounting processes."

"I hope I'm not calling at an inconvenient time." (Chapter 12)

Definition: Shows awareness of time zones in international business

Example: "Good morning. I hope I'm not calling at an inconvenient time."

"I hope this aligns with your expectations." (Chapter 12)

Definition: Shows consideration for different cultural expectations

Example: "I've prepared a detailed timeline. I hope this aligns with your expectations."

"I hope this email finds you well." (Chapter 3)

Definition: Polite, professional email opening

Example: "Dear Mr. Johnson, I hope this email finds you well."

"I'd like to see..." (Chapter 6)

Definition: Positive way to suggest improvements in feedback

Example: "I'd like to see more detailed analysis in your next report."

"I'd like to suggest..." (Chapter 4)

Definition: Clear way to introduce ideas in meetings

Example: "I'd like to suggest we run a pilot program first."

"I'd love the opportunity to..." (Chapter 7)

Definition: Shows enthusiasm for specific job responsibilities

Example: "I'd love the opportunity to lead the international expansion."

"I'd love to continue our conversation over coffee." (Chapter 8)

Definition: Natural way to suggest follow-up meetings

Example: "I'd love to continue our conversation over coffee next week."

"I'd love to learn more about how things work in [country/region]." (Chapter 12)

Definition: Shows interest in understanding cultural differences

Example: "I'd love to learn more about how things work in the German market."

"I'd love to learn more about your experience with..." (Chapter 8)

Definition: Shows respect for someone's expertise while networking

Example: "I'd love to learn more about your experience with digital transformation."

"I'll be away from my computer for the next hour." (Chapter 13)

Definition: Communicates availability status to remote colleagues

Example: "I'll be away from my computer for the next hour for a client meeting."

"I'll come back to that at the end." (Chapter 9)

Definition: Defers questions to maintain presentation flow

Example: "That's a great question. I'll come back to that when we discuss implementation."

"I'll follow up with the details in an email." (Chapter 13)

Definition: Ensures information isn't lost due to technical issues

Example: "The connection was spotty. I'll follow up with the details in an email."

"I'll send a calendar invitation with the time in all relevant time zones." (Chapter 12)

Definition: Prevents confusion in international scheduling

Example: "I'll send a calendar invitation with the time in all relevant time zones."

"I'll send you a quick message in chat." (Chapter 13)

Definition: Indicates use of instant messaging for brief communication

Example: "I'll send you a quick message in chat with that information."

"I'll share this document with editing access." (Chapter 13)

Definition: Explains collaboration permissions for shared documents

Example: "I'll share this document with editing access so everyone can contribute."

"I'll update the status in our project management tool." (Chapter 13)

Definition: Keeps remote teams informed through digital systems

Example: "I'll update the status in our project management tool after the meeting."

"I'm afraid I don't have the bandwidth right now." (Chapter 6)

Definition: Professional way to decline due to workload constraints

Example: "That sounds interesting, but I'm afraid I don't have the bandwidth right now."

"I'm confident that..." (Chapter 2)

Definition: Shows strong belief in outcomes or team abilities

Example: "I'm confident that we can deliver this project on time."

"I'm counting on you to..." (Chapter 10)

Definition: Shows trust while creating personal responsibility

Example: "Sarah, I'm counting on you to lead the client presentation."

"I'm curious about..." (Chapter 7)

Definition: Natural way to introduce questions showing genuine interest

Example: "I'm curious about the team dynamics and collaboration style."

"I'm excited to share with you..." (Chapter 9)

Definition: Shows enthusiasm and creates anticipation in presentations

Example: "I'm excited to share with you our quarterly results and future plans."

"I'm glad you brought that up." (Chapter 9)

Definition: Shows appreciation for relevant audience questions

Example: "I'm glad you brought that up. Security is indeed a major consideration."

"I'm going to mute myself while you're speaking." (Chapter 13)

Definition: Shows consideration for audio quality in virtual meetings

Example: "I'm going to mute myself while you're speaking to avoid background noise."

"I'm having some technical difficulties. Bear with me for a moment." (Chapter 13)

Definition: Acknowledges technical problems while asking for patience

Example: "I'm having some technical difficulties. Bear with me while I reconnect."

"I'm particularly proud of..." (Chapter 7)

Definition: Confident way to highlight achievements in interviews

Example: "I'm particularly proud of the retention program I developed."

"I'm proud of what we've accomplished." (Chapter 10)

Definition: Shows personal investment in team success

Example: "I'm proud of what we've accomplished this quarter."

"I'm thrilled to be here." (Chapter 7)

Definition: Shows genuine enthusiasm in professional settings

Example: "I'm thrilled to be here and learn more about this opportunity."

"I'm writing to..." (Chapter 3)

Definition: Direct way to state email purpose in opening sentence

Example: "I'm writing to inquire about the status of our proposal."

"I miss our in-person brainstorming sessions." (Chapter 13)

Definition: Acknowledges challenges of remote work positively

Example: "I miss our in-person brainstorming sessions, but we can still be creative virtually."

"I might be able to help with that." (Chapter 8)

Definition: Generous offer showing value-first networking approach

Example: "You mentioned social media challenges. I might be able to help with that."

"I need you to own this." (Chapter 10)

Definition: Clearly assigns ownership and accountability

Example: "Customer satisfaction is declining. Mike, I need you to own this issue."

"I respect that you may need time to consider this." (Chapter 12)

Definition: Acknowledges different decision-making processes across cultures

Example: "This is significant. I respect that you may need time to consider this."

"I see your point, but..." (Chapter 4)

Definition: Diplomatic way to acknowledge before disagreeing

Example: "I see your point about cost, but we should also consider quality."

"I think we both want..." (Chapter 11)

Definition: Identifies shared goals in negotiations

Example: "I think we both want a solution that creates long-term value."

"I think we have a deal." (Chapter 11)

Definition: Confident statement signaling agreement has been reached

Example: "With those modifications, I think we have a deal."

"I thought you might find this interesting..." (Chapter 8)

Definition: Valuable way to maintain relationships by sharing insights

Example: "I thought you might find this article about AI trends interesting."

"I trust your judgment on..." (Chapter 10)

Definition: Empowers team members to make decisions in their expertise area

Example: "I trust your judgment on the technical approach for this project."

"I understand business practices may be different in your country." (Chapter 12)

Definition: Acknowledges cultural differences in business approaches

Example: "I understand business practices may be different in your country. Could you guide me?"

"I understand your frustration." (Chapter 6)

Definition: Empathetic response that validates emotions without taking blame

Example: "I understand your frustration with the delays. Let's find a solution."

"I understand your position." (Chapter 11)

Definition: Shows empathy for the other party's perspective in negotiations

Example: "I understand your position on the timeline constraints."

"I want to be very clear about..." (Chapter 12)

Definition: Emphasizes important points that must be understood correctly

Example: "I want to be very clear about the delivery terms and location."

"I want to emphasize that..." (Chapter 9)

Definition: Draws attention to critical points in presentations

Example: "I want to emphasize that this change requires everyone's cooperation."

"I want to make sure I understand..." (Chapter 4)

Definition: Respectful way to ask for clarification in meetings

Example: "I want to make sure I understand the timeline correctly."

"I want to make sure I'm following proper protocol." (Chapter 12)

Definition: Shows respect for local business customs

Example: "I want to make sure I'm following proper protocol for this presentation."

"I was wondering if you could..." (Chapter 1)

Definition: Polite, indirect way to frame requests

Example: "I was wondering if you could review this document when convenient."

"I was wondering if you've had a chance to..." (Chapter 3)

Definition: Indirect way to ask for updates on previous requests

Example: "I was wondering if you've had a chance to review the contract."

"I wish I could help, but..." (Chapter 6)

Definition: Sympathetic way to decline while showing genuine desire to help

Example: "I wish I could help, but I'm committed to another project this month."

"I work with [industry/type of client] to [solve specific problem]." (Chapter 8)

Definition: Value-focused self-introduction emphasizing problem-solving

Example: "I work with tech startups to develop effective marketing strategies."

"If we stick to the timeline..." (Chapter 5)

Definition: Discusses outcomes based on maintaining current schedule

Example: "If we stick to the timeline, we'll have the prototype ready next month."

"I'm glad you brought that up." (Chapter 9)

Definition: Shows appreciation for relevant questions or comments

Example: "I'm glad you brought that up. That's exactly what we need to address."

"In exchange for..." (Chapter 11)

Definition: Links concessions to reciprocal benefits in negotiations

Example: "In exchange for the volume discount, we'd need a minimum order commitment."

"In my experience..." (Chapter 7)

Definition: Strong way to begin examples demonstrating relevant experience

Example: "In my experience, customer retention improves with personalized service."

"In my previous role..." (Chapter 7)

Definition: Professional way to reference past experience and achievements

Example: "In my previous role, I increased team productivity by 30%."

"In short..." (Chapter 2)

Definition: Summarizes complex ideas to get to the main point quickly

Example: "The analysis is detailed, but in short, we're seeing strong growth."

"Is now a good time for a quick call?" (Chapter 13)

Definition: Respects others' schedules before initiating unscheduled calls

Example: "I have a question about the project. Is now a good time for a quick call?"

"Is there any flexibility on...?" (Chapter 11)

Definition: Polite way to test if terms are negotiable

Example: "Is there any flexibility on the delivery timeline?"

"It was great meeting you at [event]." (Chapter 8) Definition: Warm way to begin follow-up messages after networking

Example: "It was great meeting you at the Marketing Summit last week."

"It would be great if..." (Chapter 6)

Definition: Positive way to suggest improvements in feedback

Example: "It would be great if you could include more supporting data."

"It's a pleasure to meet you." (Chapter 1)

Definition: Professional and warm greeting for first-time meetings

Example: "Hello, I'm Sarah from Marketing. It's a pleasure to meet you."

"I've attached..." (Chapter 3)

Definition: Modern way to reference email attachments

Example: "I've attached the meeting agenda for your review."

"I've been looking forward to this conversation." (Chapter 7)

Definition: Shows engagement and preparation for meetings

Example: "I've been looking forward to this conversation about the position."

"I've heard great things about your work." (Chapter 1)

Definition: Sincere compliment showing you've done research

Example: "I've heard great things about your work on the software launch."

"I've noticed that..." (Chapter 6)

Definition: Neutral way to begin feedback focusing on specific behaviors

Example: "I've noticed that the last few reports were submitted late."

"I've observed that..." (Chapter 6)

Definition: Factual way to introduce feedback based on specific observations

Example: "I've observed that team meetings often run over the scheduled time."

J

"Just a gentle reminder that..." (Chapter 3)

Definition: Polite way to send follow-up reminders

Example: "Just a gentle reminder that the proposal is due tomorrow."

K

"I know it's early/late for you." (Chapter 12)

Definition: Acknowledges inconvenience of time zone differences

Example: "Thank you for joining. I know it's quite early for you in Sydney."

L

"Let me address that in two parts..." (Chapter 9)

Definition: Organizes complex answers to multifaceted questions

Example: "Let me address that in two parts: the technical requirements and the timeline."

"Let me give you a concrete example..." (Chapter 9)

Definition: Introduces real-world examples to illustrate abstract concepts

Example: "Let me give you a concrete example of how this process works."

"Let me just repeat that back to you to make sure I have it right." (Chapter 2)

Definition: Thorough way to confirm important details or instructions

Example: "Let me just repeat that back: you need the report by Friday at 3 PM."

"Let me make sure I understand correctly..." (Chapter 12)

Definition: Crucial phrase for preventing international communication misunderstandings

Example: "Let me make sure I understand correctly—you need delivery by month-end?"

"Let me start with a question..." (Chapter 9)

Definition: Interactive way to begin presentations that engages audience

Example: "Let me start with a question: How many of you use our mobile app?"

"Let's brainstorm some alternatives." (Chapter 5)

Definition: Invites creative thinking to generate multiple solutions

Example: "The original plan isn't working. Let's brainstorm some alternatives."

"Let's explore some options." (Chapter 11)

Definition: Suggests collaborative problem-solving in negotiations

Example: "We have different priorities. Let's explore some options that work for both."

"Let's find a solution that works for everyone." (Chapter 6)

Definition: Collaborative phrase shifting focus from blame to problem-solving

Example: "We have different needs here. Let's find a solution that works for everyone."

"Let's focus on what we can control." (Chapter 10)

Definition: Redirects energy from external worries to productive action

Example: "The market is uncertain, but let's focus on what we can control."

"Let's go around the room and hear from everyone." (Chapter 13)

Definition: Ensures all participants contribute in virtual meetings

Example: "Before we conclude, let's go around the room and hear from everyone."

"Let's move forward with this." (Chapter 11)

Definition: Decisive phrase transitioning from negotiation to implementation

Example: "This proposal addresses our concerns. Let's move forward with this."

"Let's put our heads together." (Chapter 5)

Definition: Encourages collaborative thinking and problem-solving

Example: "This is complex. Let's put our heads together and find a solution."

"Let's schedule some time to catch up properly." (Chapter 13)

Definition: Suggests dedicated time for relationship building beyond work

Example: "We've been so busy. Let's schedule some time to catch up properly."

"Let's set up a shared workspace for this project." (Chapter 13)

Definition: Suggests centralized location for remote team collaboration

Example: "Let's set up a shared workspace where we can store all project files."

"Let's take a step back." (Chapter 6)

Definition: Pauses heated discussions to refocus on core issues

Example: "We're getting caught up in details. Let's take a step back."

"Let me know if you'd prefer to discuss this over video call." (Chapter 13)

Definition: Offers to escalate from text to face-to-face virtual interaction

Example: "This email is getting long. Let me know if you'd prefer to discuss over video call."

M

"Moving forward..." (Chapter 6)

Definition: Shifts conversation from past problems to future solutions

Example: "There were challenges last quarter. Moving forward, let's establish clearer checkpoints."

"My thinking on this is..." (Chapter 2)

Definition: Confident way to introduce opinions while remaining collaborative

Example: "My thinking on this is that we should prioritize user experience first."

N

"No worries if not." (Chapter 1)

Definition: Takes pressure off requests and shows respect for others' priorities

Example: "Could you review this? No worries if not—I know you're busy."

"Now that we've covered..., let's move on to..." (Chapter 9)

Definition: Clear transition maintaining flow between presentation sections

Example: "Now that we've covered the challenges, let's move on to solutions."

O

"Our priority right now is..." (Chapter 10)

Definition: Provides clear focus during uncertain times

Example: "There's market uncertainty. Our priority right now is customer retention."

P

"Please correct me if I'm mispronouncing your name." (Chapter 12)

Definition: Shows respect for cultural identity and desire to get names right

Example: "Nice to meet you, Ms. Kowalski. Please correct me if I'm mispronouncing your name."

"Please don't hesitate to reach out if..." (Chapter 8)

Definition: Generous closing leaving door open for future collaboration

Example: "Please don't hesitate to reach out if you have marketing questions."

"Please feel free to interrupt if you have questions." (Chapter 12)

Definition: Encourages participation from cultures where interrupting seems rude

Example: "I'll present for 20 minutes. Please feel free to interrupt if you have questions."

"Please find attached..." (Chapter 3)

Definition: Standard way to reference email attachments

Example: "Please find attached the meeting agenda for tomorrow's session."

"Please let me know if there's a better way to approach this." (Chapter 12)

Definition: Shows openness to different business practices

Example: "I've outlined our standard terms. Please let me know if there's a better approach."

S

"Should we find a time that's more convenient for everyone?" (Chapter 12)

Definition: Suggests finding meeting times that work better across time zones

Example: "This 6 AM call is challenging. Should we find a more convenient time?"

"Should we try calling in by phone instead?" (Chapter 13)

Definition: Suggests alternative when video connection issues persist

Example: "The video keeps freezing. Should we try calling in by phone instead?"

"So, if I understand correctly..." (Chapter 2)

Definition: Best way to confirm understanding by restating in your own words

Example: "So, if I understand correctly, you need the draft by tomorrow?"

"So, if I understand correctly, we're agreeing to..." (Chapter 11)

Definition: Summarizes key agreement points before finalizing

Example: "So, if I understand correctly, we're agreeing to a 12-month contract with quarterly reviews."

"So, what do you do at [Company Name]?" (Chapter 1)

Definition: Direct but polite way to understand someone's role

Example: "It's great to meet you, Maria. So, what do you do at Apex Solutions?"

T

"Thanks for making the time to meet with me." (Chapter 1)

Definition: Polite way to open meetings acknowledging others' valuable time

Example: "Good morning, Ms. Chen. Thanks for making the time to meet with me."

"That aligns perfectly with my experience in..." (Chapter 7)

Definition: Connects your background to what employers are seeking

Example: "That aligns perfectly with my experience in digital marketing campaigns."

"That makes perfect sense from your perspective." (Chapter 11)

Definition: Validates reasoning without necessarily agreeing with conclusions

Example: "That makes perfect sense from your perspective as CFO."

"That's a great question." (Chapter 2)

Definition: Classic response to difficult questions that buys thinking time

Example: "How will this affect existing clients? That's a great question."

"That's a great question. Let me think about that for a moment." (Chapter 7)

Definition: Buys time for thoughtful responses to unexpected questions

Example: "That's a great question about handling difficult situations. Let me think about that."

"That's an excellent question." (Chapter 9)

Definition: Positive response validating questioners in presentations

Example: "What about implementation costs? That's an excellent question."

"That's exactly my thinking." (Chapter 4)

Definition: Conversational way to show strong agreement

Example: "We should focus mobile-first. That's exactly my thinking."

"That's fascinating. Tell me more about..." (Chapter 8)

Definition: Shows genuine interest encouraging others to share details

Example: "That's fascinating. Tell me more about your AI implementation."

"That's outside my area of expertise." (Chapter 6)

Definition: Honest way to decline when you're not the right person

Example: "That's outside my area of expertise. Try the IT department."

"That's something I'd have to think about." (Chapter 11)

Definition: Buys time to consider offers without rejecting outright

Example: "A 20% discount is significant. That's something I'd have to think about."

"The bottom line is..." (Chapter 2)

Definition: Direct phrase for stating the most important conclusion

Example: "We can discuss strategies all day, but the bottom line is we need 10% growth."

"The deadline is tight, but doable." (Chapter 5)

Definition: Acknowledges time pressure while expressing confidence

Example: "The client wants this Friday. The deadline is tight, but doable."

"The key takeaway here is..." (Chapter 9)

Definition: Highlights most important points from presentation sections

Example: "We've looked at several approaches. The key takeaway is automation gives the best ROI."

"The next steps are..." (Chapter 9)

Definition: Provides clear direction for post-presentation action

Example: "The next steps are budget approval Friday and team formation next week."

"The success of this project depends on..." (Chapter 10)

Definition: Clearly communicates what's most critical for success

Example: "The success of this project depends on clear client communication and staying within budget."

"The way I see it..." (Chapter 11)

Definition: Presents perspective as one valid viewpoint among others

Example: "The way I see it, this partnership could help both companies expand faster."

"The bottleneck is..." (Chapter 5)

Definition: Business term identifying what's slowing down progress

Example: "Everything's ready except legal approval. The bottleneck is the legal team."

"This brings me to my next point..." (Chapter 9)

Definition: Smooth transition showing logical progression in presentations

Example: "Customer retention improved significantly. This brings me to my next point about expansion."

"This is exactly the kind of thinking we need." (Chapter 10)

Definition: Reinforces specific behaviors you want to see more of

Example: "Sarah's customer-first suggestion is exactly the kind of thinking we need."

"This is our opportunity to..." (Chapter 10)

Definition: Frames challenges as opportunities for positive action

Example: "The market downturn is challenging, but this is our opportunity to gain market share."

"This is particularly important because..." (Chapter 9)

Definition: Emphasizes significance helping audience understand importance

Example: "This affects not just our department, but the entire customer experience. This is particularly important because..."

"This would be right up your alley." (Chapter 5)

Definition: Encouraging way to assign tasks matching someone's skills

Example: "We need UX design work. Lisa, this would be right up your alley."

"Thank you all for being here today." (Chapter 9)

Definition: Warm, appreciative presentation opening creating positive atmosphere

Example: "Thank you all for being here today. I know how busy everyone is."

"Thank you for taking the time to meet with me today." (Chapter 7)

Definition: Professional and gracious interview opening

Example: "Good morning, Ms. Johnson. Thank you for taking the time to meet with me today."

"Thank you for your attention. I'm happy to take any questions." (Chapter 9)

Definition: Professional presentation closing opening floor for discussion

Example: "That concludes my presentation. Thank you for your attention. I'm happy to take questions."

"To avoid any confusion..." (Chapter 12)

Definition: Proactively addresses potential misunderstandings with clarity

Example: "To avoid any confusion, when I say 'next week,' I mean March 15th."

"To be clear..." (Chapter 2)

Definition: Adds emphasis before stating something requiring no misunderstanding

Example: "We can meet the deadline. But to be clear, everyone works Saturday."

"To put it simply..." (Chapter 2)

Definition: Summarizes complex ideas to get to main point quickly

Example: "The analysis is detailed, but to put it simply, we're seeing growth."

"To put this in perspective..." (Chapter 9)

Definition: Helps audience understand significance or context of information

Example: "We saved 30 seconds per transaction. To put this in perspective, that's 200 hours monthly."

"To summarize the key points..." (Chapter 9)

Definition: Signals wrap-up while reinforcing main messages

Example: "To summarize the key points: we identified the problem, explored solutions, and recommended the best approach."

W

"We need a workaround." (Chapter 5)

Definition: Indicates need for alternative when ideal solution unavailable

Example: "The software isn't available until next month. We need a workaround."

"We need to push back the deadline." (Chapter 5)

Definition: Direct communication that deadline cannot be met

Example: "Given the scope changes, we need to push back the deadline by one week."

"We're cutting it close." (Chapter 5)

Definition: Honest way to say timing will be very tight

Example: "We're cutting it close with the presentation deadline."

"We're going to make a real difference here." (Chapter 10)

Definition: Connects team's work to larger purpose and meaning

Example: "This customer service initiative isn't just about metrics. We're going to make a real difference."

"We're on the same side here." (Chapter 11)

Definition: Reinforces collaborative rather than adversarial approach

Example: "We're on the same side here. We both want this project to succeed."

"We're on track to..." (Chapter 5) Definition:

Positive way to report progress toward specific goals

Example: "The development phase is going well. We're on track to complete the beta next week."

"We'll figure this out together." (Chapter 10)

Definition: Creates unity and shared problem-solving during challenges

Example: "This is complex and I don't have all answers. But we'll figure this out together."

"We've hit a snag with..." (Chapter 5)

Definition: Professional way to report problems without being overly dramatic

Example: "We've hit a snag with the database integration, but the vendor is working on a fix."

"What are the biggest challenges facing the team right now?" (Chapter 7)

Definition: Strategic interview question showing forward-thinking

Example: "What are the biggest challenges facing the team? I'd love to understand where I could make immediate impact."

"What brings you to [event/conference]?" (Chapter 8)

Definition: Great follow-up question after introductions leading to meaningful conversation

Example: "Nice to meet you, David. What brings you to the Digital Marketing Summit?"

"What did we learn from this?" (Chapter 10)

Definition: Turns mistakes and setbacks into learning opportunities

Example: "The launch didn't go smoothly. What did we learn that we can apply next time?"

"What do you think we should do?" (Chapter 10)

Definition: Encourages strategic thinking and ownership rather than just following orders

Example: "We're behind schedule. What do you think we should do to get back on track?"

"What does success look like in this role?" (Chapter 7)

Definition: Strategic interview question understanding expectations and showing results focus

Example: "What does success look like in this role after the first six months?"

"What I found particularly rewarding was…" (Chapter 7)

Definition: Highlights achievements while showing what motivates you

Example: "What I found particularly rewarding was mentoring junior team members."

"What if we…?" (Chapter 4)

Definition: Collaborative way to propose alternatives inviting discussion

Example: "What if we approached this from the customer's perspective instead?"

"What if we could…" (Chapter 11)

Definition: Introduces creative solutions in hypothetical, non-threatening way

Example: "What if we could reduce upfront costs while meeting quality requirements?"

"What matters most to you in this deal?" (Chapter 11)

Definition: Uncovers other party's priorities for better offer structuring

Example: "What matters most to you—the price, timeline, or ongoing support?"

"What time works best for you in your time zone?" (Chapter 12)

Definition: Shows consideration for others' local time rather than assuming accommodation

Example: "I'd like to schedule a call. What time works best for you in your time zone?"

"What would be the most appropriate way to...?" (Chapter 12)

Definition: Asks for guidance on cultural or business protocols

Example: "What would be the most appropriate way to follow up on this proposal?"

"What would it take for you to...?" (Chapter 11)

Definition: Powerful question uncovering real needs and constraints

Example: "What would it take for you to consider extending the contract another year?"

"What's our best option here?" (Chapter 5)

Definition: Focuses team on finding practical solutions rather than dwelling on problems

Example: "The original plan isn't working. What's our best option here?"

"Would you be able to...?" (Chapter 1)

Definition: Gentle, professional way to ask for help giving easy decline option

Example: "Would you be able to look over this presentation? I'd appreciate a second opinion."

Y

"You have my full support on this." (Chapter 10)

Definition: Assures team members you'll provide resources and backing needed

Example: "This is challenging, but you have my full support. Let me know what you need."

"You're absolutely right." (Chapter 6)

Definition: Straightforward way to accept valid criticism showing accountability

Example: "You're absolutely right. I should have consulted the team first."

"You've set a new standard for..." (Chapter 10)

Definition: Recognizes exceptional performance while setting future expectations

Example: "Tom, you've set a new standard for customer service excellence."

CHAPTER FIFTEEN

Interactive Learning Section (Bonus)

Put your business English skills to the test with realistic scenarios and practice exercises

How to Use This Section

This interactive section is designed to help you practice and reinforce everything you've learned from the book. It includes realistic business scenarios, self-assessment quizzes, and common mistake correction exercises. Work through these at your own pace, and don't worry about getting everything perfect the first time—the goal is to build confidence through practice.

Recommended Approach:

1. Complete the scenarios first to practice in realistic contexts

2. Take the self-assessment quizzes to identify areas for improvement

3. Work through the mistake correction exercises to avoid common pitfalls

4. Review your answers using the provided answer keys

Part A: Realistic Business Scenarios

Scenario 1: The New Client Presentation

Background: You work for a marketing agency and are meeting with a potential new client, TechFlow Industries, for the first time. The client has expressed interest in your services but is also considering two other agencies. You need to make a strong first impression, understand their needs, and position your agency as the best choice.

Your Role: Senior Account Manager **Setting:** Video conference call **Participants:** You, Sarah Chen (TechFlow CMO), and David Park (TechFlow Marketing Director)

Part 1: Opening the Meeting You're joining the call and need to:

- Greet the participants professionally
- Acknowledge any technical setup
- Set the tone for a productive conversation

Your Response: *Write how you would open this meeting using expressions from the book.*

Part 2: Understanding Their Needs Sarah mentions: "We've been struggling with our digital marketing ROI. Our current campaigns aren't generating the leads we need, and we're not sure if it's a strategy issue or an execution problem."

Your Response: *How would you respond to show you're listening and gather more information?*

Part 3: Presenting Your Solution After understanding their challenges, you need to present your agency's approach without being too sales-heavy.

Your Response: *How would you introduce your solution in a collaborative way?*

Part 4: Handling Objections David says: "Your approach sounds good, but your pricing is about 20% higher than the other agencies we're considering. How do you justify that?"

Your Response: *How would you address this pricing concern diplomatically?*

Part 5: Closing the Meeting The meeting has gone well, and you want to establish clear next steps.

Your Response: *How would you close the meeting and set up follow-up actions?*

Scenario 2: The Difficult Team Meeting

Background: You're leading a project that's running behind schedule. Team morale is low, there have been some conflicts between team members, and your manager is asking for daily updates. You need to address the issues while keeping the team motivated and finding solutions.

Your Role: Project Manager **Setting:** In-person team meeting **Participants:** You and five team members (Alex, Maria, Tom, Jennifer, and Sam)

Part 1: Addressing the Elephant in the Room Everyone knows the project is behind schedule and tensions are high.

Your Response: *How would you open the meeting to acknowledge the challenges while maintaining a positive outlook?*

Part 2: Facilitating Problem-Solving You need to get the team to identify the root causes of the delays without pointing fingers.

Your Response: *What questions would you ask to encourage collaborative problem-solving?*

Part 3: Managing Conflict Alex interrupts Maria mid-sentence and says, "That's not going to work. We tried that approach last month and it was a disaster."

Your Response: *How would you handle this interruption and redirect the conversation constructively?*

Part 4: Delegating and Empowering You've identified some solutions and need to assign responsibilities while empowering team members.

Your Response: *How would you delegate tasks while showing confidence in your team?*

Part 5: Ending on a Positive Note You want to wrap up the meeting with clear action items and renewed motivation.

Your Response: *How would you close the meeting to inspire confidence and commitment?*

Scenario 3: The International Negotiation

Background: You're negotiating a partnership agreement with a Japanese company. This is your first major international deal, and you want to be respectful of cultural differences while achieving your business objectives. The negotiation has been ongoing for several weeks.

Your Role: Business Development Director **Setting:** Video conference with some participants in Tokyo, others in New York **Participants:** You, Hiroshi Tanaka (Tokyo CEO), Yuki Sato (Tokyo CFO), and your colleague James (New York)

Part 1: Opening with Cultural Sensitivity It's 9 AM in New York and 11 PM in Tokyo.

Your Response: *How would you open the meeting acknowledging the time zone challenges and showing cultural awareness?*

Part 2: Presenting Your Position You need to propose some changes to the contract terms, but you want to do so diplomatically.

Your Response: *How would you present your proposed changes without seeming demanding?*

Part 3: Understanding Their Concerns Hiroshi responds: "We appreciate your proposal, but we need to discuss this internally. In our company, decisions like this require consensus from several departments."

Your Response: *How would you respond to show respect for their decision-making process?*

Part 4: Finding Common Ground You realize you need to find areas of mutual benefit to move forward.

Your Response: *What would you say to identify shared interests and build on them?*

Part 5: Closing with Next Steps The meeting has been productive, but no final decisions have been made.

Your Response: *How would you close the meeting while respecting their need for internal discussion?*

Part B: Self-Assessment Quizzes

Quiz 1: Email Communication

Instructions: Choose the most professional and effective option for each situation.

Question 1: You need to follow up on an email you sent a week ago that hasn't been answered. Which opening is best?

A) "I'm writing again because you didn't respond to my last email." B) "Just a gentle reminder that I'm still waiting for your response." C) "I was wondering if you've had a chance to review my previous email about the project proposal." D) "Please respond to my email immediately as this is urgent."

A) "I can't make it to the meeting." B) "I'm afraid I don't have the bandwidth for the meeting on Tuesday." C) "Sorr, but I'm too busy that day." D) "I wish I could attend, but I have a conflict on Tuesday. Could we explore alternative times?"

Question 3: You're attaching a document to an email. Which phrase is most appropriate?

A) "I'm sending you the file." B) "Please find attached the quarterly report for your review." C) "The document is attached to this email." D) "Here's the file you wanted."

Quiz 2: Meeting Participation

Question 1: A colleague presents an idea you disagree with. What's the most diplomatic response?

A) "That won't work because..." B) "I disagree with that approach." C) "I see your point, but I have a slightly different perspective on this." D) "That's wrong. We should do it this way instead."

Question 2: You want to ask for clarification on a complex topic. Which approach is best?

A) "I don't understand what you're talking about." B) "Could you elaborate on that? I want to make sure I understand the implications." C) "That doesn't make sense to me." D) "Can you explain tha again?"

Question 3: You want to contribute an idea to the discussion. How should you introduce it?

) "I think we should..." B) "The right way to do this is..." C) "I'd like to suggest we consider..." D) "We need to..."

Quiz 3: Leadership Communication

uestion 1: Your team is facing a challenging deadline. How

A) "We have to work harder to meet this deadline." B) "I have complete confidence in this team. This is our opportunity to show what we can accomplish." C) "If we don't meet this deadline, we'll be in trouble." D) "Everyone needs to put in extra hours this week."

Question 2: You need to delegate an important task. Which approach is most empowering?

A) "I need you to handle the client presentation." B) "You're responsible for the client presentation." C) "I'm counting on you to lead the client presentation. You have my full support." D) "Make sure you don't mess up the client presentation."

Question 3: A project has encountered unexpected problems. How do you address the team

Part C: Common Mistake Correctionxercise 1: Email Mistakes

Instructions: Identify what's wrong with each email excerpt and rewrite it professional

Mistake 1: *"Hey guys, just wanted to touch base about the thing we discussed. Can you get back to me ASAP? Thx!"*

What's Wrong:

- Too casual ("Hey guys")

- Vague reference ("the thing")

- Unclear request

- Unprofessional abbreviations

Corrected Version: *"Good morning team, I wanted to follow up on our discussion about the marketing budget allocation. Could you please send me your department's requirements by Friday? I appreciate your prompt response."*

Mistake 2: *"I need you to send me the report immediately. This is urgent and I can't wait any longer."*

What's Wrong:

- Too demanding

- No politeness

- Creates unnecessary pressure

Corrected Version: *"I was wondering if you could prioritize the quarterly report? We have a client meeting tomorrow and would greatly appreciate having it by end of day today. Please let me know if this timeline works for you."*

Exercise 2: Meeting Mistakes

Mistake 1: *"That's a stupid idea and it will never work."*

What's Wrong:

- Personal attack

- Completely negative
- Shuts down discussion

Corrected Version: *"I see your point, but I have concerns about the implementation. Have we considered the potential challenges with this approach?"*

Mistake 2: *"Um, well, I think, you know, maybe we could, like, try a different approach?"*

What's Wrong:

- Too many filler words
- Sounds uncertain
- Lacks confidence

Corrected Version: *"I'd like to suggest we consider an alternative approach. What if we focused on the customer experience first?"*

Exercise 3: Presentation Mistakes

Mistake 1: *"So, um, today I'm going to talk about, you know, our sales numbers and stuff."*

What's Wrong:

- Filler words
- Vague language

- Unprofessional tone

Corrected Version: *"Thank you all for being here today. I'm excited to share our Q3 sales results and discuss what they mean for our Q4 strategy."*

Mistake 2: *"I don't know if this will work, but maybe we could try this idea."*

What's Wrong:

- Shows lack of confidence
- Tentative language
- Doesn't inspire confidence

Corrected Version: *"I'm confident this approach will deliver results. Let me walk you through how we can implement this strategy."*

Part D: Answer Keys and Explanations

Scenario Answer Guidelines

Scenario 1 - Sample Responses:

Part 1: "Good morning, Sarah and David. Thank you for taking the time to meet with me today. I can see everyone clearly—are you able to hear me okay? I'm excited to learn more about TechFlow's marketing goals and explore how we might work together."

Part 2: "That's exactly the kind of challenge we help companies solve. Could you elaborate on what you mean by ROI issues? Are you seeing low conversion rates, high cost per lead, or both? I'd love to understand the specific metrics you're tracking."

Part 3: "Based on what you've told me about your challenges, here's what I'm thinking. We specialize in helping tech companies like yours optimize their digital marketing ROI through data-driven strategy and precise execution. What if we could show you exactly where your current campaigns are losing effectiveness?"

Part 4: "I understand your position on pricing—budget is always a key consideration. The way I see it, our higher fee reflects the additional value we provide through our specialized expertise and proven results. What matters most to you in this partnership—the initial cost or the long-term ROI improvement?"

Part 5: "This has been a productive conversation. Based on what we've discussed, I believe we can help TechFlow achieve its marketing goals. The next steps would be for me to prepare a detailed proposal addressing your specific challenges. Are we in agreement that I should have this to you by Friday?"

Quiz Answer Keys

Quiz 1 - Email Communication:

1. C - Professional, polite, and specific

2. D - Shows regret, explains briefly, offers alternatives

3. B - Professional standard phrase with clear purpose

Quiz 2 - Meeting Participation:

1. B - Shows engagement and desire to understand fully

2. C - Professional way to introduce ideas for discussion

Quiz 3 - Leadership Communication:

1. B - Shows confidence in team and frames challenge positively

2. C - Empowering language with support assurance

3. B - Transparent and collaborative approach to problems

Part E: Practice Exercises for Continued Learning

Daily Practice Suggestions

Week 1: Email Excellence

- Day 1-2: Practice professional email openings
- Day 3-4: Work on polite request language
- Day 5-7: Focus on clear, concise closings

Week 2: Meeting Mastery

- Day 1-2: Practice agreeing and building on ideas
- Day 3-4: Work on diplomatic disagreement
- Day 5-7: Focus on asking clarifying questions

Week 3: Presentation Power

- Day 1-2: Practice engaging openings
- Day 3-4: Work on smooth transitions
- Day 5-7: Focus on confident closings

Week 4: Leadership Language

- Day 1-2: Practice motivational phrases
- Day 3-4: Work on empowering delegation
- Day 5-7: Focus on problem-solving language

Self-Reflection Questions

After completing these exercises, ask yourself:

1. Which expressions feel most natural to me now?

2. What situations still make me feel uncertain about word choice?

3. How has my confidence in professional communication improved?

4. Which areas need more practice?

5. How can I incorporate these expressions into my daily work?

Next Steps for Continued Growth

1. **Record Yourself:** Practice key expressions by recording yourself and listening back

2. **Role-Play:** Practice scenarios with colleagues or friends

3. **Real-World Application:** Use one new expression each day in actual work situations

4. **Feedback Seeking:** Ask trusted colleagues for feedback on your communication

5. **Continuous Learning:** Keep this book as a reference and review regularly

Remember: Mastering business English is a journey, not a destination. The more you practice these expressions in real situations, the more natural and confident you'll become. Use this interactive section as often as needed to build and maintain your skills.

CHAPTER SIXTEEN

Your Journey Toward Mastery

Transforming knowledge into lasting professional success

Congratulations! You've completed a comprehensive journey through the essential expressions and phrases that define professional business communication. From building your first professional relationships to leading international negotiations, from crafting compelling emails to delivering powerful presentations, you now have a toolkit of over 150 proven expressions that can transform how you communicate in any business setting.

But this book's end is really just the beginning of your journey to true mastery.

What You've Accomplished

Take a moment to appreciate how far you've come. When you started this book, you may have felt uncertain about the right words to use in challenging professional situations. Now, you have:

✓ **A Foundation of Confidence** You understand that effective business communication isn't about using the most complex vocabulary—it's about choosing the right expression for each situation. You've learned that a simple phrase like "I see your point, but..." can transform a potential conflict into a productive discussion.

✓ **Cultural Awareness** You recognize that business communication varies across cultures and contexts. Whether you're working with international colleagues or adapting to virtual environments, you now have the sensitivity and language skills to navigate these differences successfully.

✓ **Situational Fluency** You've mastered expressions for every major business scenario: building relationships, managing projects, handling difficult conversations, leading teams, negotiating deals, and presenting ideas. You're no longer searching for the right words—you have them at your fingertips.

✓ **Professional Presence** Perhaps most importantly, you've developed the language that projects competence, confidence, and leadership. You know how to disagree diplomatically, delegate empoweringly, and inspire others through your words.

The Key Principles That Will Serve You Forever

As you continue your professional journey, remember these fundamental principles that underpin all effective business communication:

1. Clarity Over Complexity

The most powerful business communication is often the simplest. "The bottom line is..." will always be more effective than a paragraph of jargon. Your goal is to be understood, not to impress with vocabulary.

2. Respect Before Results

Every expression in this book is built on a foundation of respect—for others' time, perspectives, expertise, and cultural differences. When you show respect through your language choices, people are more likely to listen, collaborate, and support your ideas.

3. Collaboration Over Competition

The most successful professionals use language that builds bridges, not walls. Phrases like "Let's put our heads together" and "We're on the same side here" create partnerships that achieve far more than individual effort ever could.

4. Confidence With Humility

True professional confidence isn't about having all the answers—it's about being comfortable with phrases like "That's a great question" and "I'd love to learn more about your experience." Confident professionals know when to lead and when to listen.

5. Authenticity in Every Interaction

The expressions in this book work because they reflect genuine human connection. Don't just memorize phrases—internalize the mindset behind them. When you genuinely care about understanding others and adding value, the right words will follow naturally.

Your Roadmap for Continued Growth

Mastering business English is not a destination—it's an ongoing journey of growth and refinement. Here's your roadmap for continued improvement:

Phase 1: Integration (Months 1-3)

Goal: Make these expressions feel natural and automatic

Daily Practice:

- Choose one new expression each day and use it in a real work situation

- Keep the Thematic Quick-Reference Glossary accessible during meetings and calls

- Practice the Interactive Learning scenarios once per week

Weekly Focus:

- Week 1-2: Master email and written communication expressions

- Week 3-4: Focus on meeting participation and discussion phrases

- Week 5-6: Practice presentation and public speaking language

- Week 7-8: Work on leadership and delegation expressions

- Week 9-10: Develop negotiation and persuasion skills

- Week 11-12: Refine international and virtual communication

Phase 2: Mastery (Months 4-6)

Goal: Adapt expressions naturally to your specific industry and role

Advanced Practice:

- Record yourself using key expressions and listen for naturalness
- Seek feedback from trusted colleagues on your communication style
- Practice handling unexpected situations with the expressions you've learned
- Begin mentoring others and teaching them effective business communication

Specialization:

- Identify the 20-30 expressions most relevant to your specific role
- Practice industry-specific variations of core expressions
- Develop your own examples and scenarios based on your work experience

Phase 3: Leadership (Months 6+)

Goal: Become a communication role model and help others improve

Leadership Development:

- Use your communication skills to facilitate better team discussions

- Help colleagues improve their own business communication

- Adapt your communication style for different audiences and situations

- Continuously refine your approach based on results and feedback

Strategies for Lifelong Learning

1. The Daily Expression Challenge

Each morning, choose one expression from this book and commit to using it naturally during the day. Keep a small notebook or phone note tracking which expressions you've practiced and how they felt in real situations.

2. The Feedback Loop

Regularly ask trusted colleagues: "How did that come across?" or "Was my message clear?" This feedback will help you calibrate your communication and identify areas for continued improvement.

3. The Observation Method

Pay attention to how effective communicators in your organization use language. Notice which expressions they use in different situations and how people respond. Model the approaches that work best in your environment.

4. The Teaching Test

The best way to master something is to teach it. Share what you've learned with colleagues, mentor junior team members, or even just explain concepts to friends and family. Teaching forces you to truly understand and internalize the material.

5. The Cultural Expansion

As you encounter new cultures, industries, or business contexts, observe how communication styles adapt. Use the principles from this book as a foundation, but remain flexible and open to learning new approaches.

Resources for Ongoing Development

Professional Development Opportunities

- **Toastmasters International:** Practice public speaking and presentation skills
- **Industry Conferences:** Observe and practice networking and professional communication
- **Professional Associations:** Engage in discussions and build relationships using your new skills
- **Online Communities:** Participate in professional forums and LinkedIn discussions

Recommended Reading

- Industry-specific communication guides for your field
- Books on cultural intelligence for international business
- Leadership communication resources as you advance in your career
- Current business publications to stay updated on communication trends

Technology Tools

- **Grammar and Style Checkers:** Tools like Grammarly for written communication
- **Presentation Software:** Master tools that enhance your verbal presentations
- **Video Conferencing Platforms:** Become proficient in virtual communication tools
- **Project Management Systems:** Learn to communicate effectively through digital platforms

Measuring Your Progress

How will you know you're succeeding? Look for these indicators:

Immediate Signs (Weeks 1-4)

- You feel more confident in meetings and professional conversations

- You spend less time searching for the right words
- Colleagues respond more positively to your emails and requests
- You handle difficult conversations with greater ease

Medium-term Indicators (Months 1-6)

- You're invited to participate in more high-level discussions
- People seek your input and value your opinions
- You successfully navigate challenging negotiations and conflicts
- Your presentations and communications receive positive feedback

Long-term Success Markers (6+ Months)

- You're recognized as an effective communicator in your organization
- You're comfortable communicating with people at all levels and from all cultures
- You help others improve their communication skills
- Your career advancement reflects your enhanced communication abilities

A Personal Message

As you close this book and continue your professional journey, remember that every expert was once a beginner. Every confident speaker once struggled to find the right words. Every successful leader once felt uncertain about how to motivate their team.

What sets successful professionals apart isn't perfection—it's the commitment to continuous improvement and the courage to practice new skills even when they feel uncomfortable at first.

You now have the tools. You understand the principles. You've practiced the scenarios. Most importantly, you have the mindset that effective communication is about serving others—helping them understand, feel heard, and work together toward common goals.

The expressions in this book will serve you well, but remember that they're just the beginning. As you grow in your career, you'll develop your own style, discover new phrases, and adapt these foundations to your unique professional context.

Your Next Steps

Before you put this book away, take these three immediate actions:

1. Choose Your Top 10 Review the Thematic Quick-Reference Glossary and identify the 10 expressions that are most relevant to your current role and challenges. Write them down and commit to mastering them first.

2. Set Your Practice Schedule Decide when and how you'll practice. Will you review expressions during your morning coffee? Practice scenarios during lunch breaks? Use new phrases in afternoon meetings? Make it specific and realistic.

3. Find Your Accountability Partner Share your communication goals with a trusted colleague, mentor, or friend. Ask them to help you practice and provide feedback on your progress.

Final Thoughts

Business English mastery isn't about memorizing phrases—it's about building bridges. Every expression you've learned is a tool for connecting with others, solving problems together, and creating value in your professional relationships.

As you use these expressions in your daily work, remember that behind every phrase is a human being who wants to be understood, respected, and valued. When you communicate with that mindset, using the professional language you've mastered in this book, you'll not only advance your own career—you'll make every workplace interaction more productive, positive, and meaningful.

The journey to mastery is ongoing, but you're no longer traveling alone. You have a comprehensive toolkit, a clear roadmap, and most importantly, the confidence to communicate effectively in any business situation.

Your professional communication journey starts now. Make it count.

Welcome to your new level of professional excellence. The business world is waiting to hear what you have to say.

"The single biggest problem in communication is the illusion that it has taken place."

— George Bernard Shaw

Don't just communicate. Connect. Don't just speak. Inspire. Don't just use words. Build bridges.

Your journey to mastery continues with every conversation, every email, every meeting, and every presentation. Make them all count.